IMPEACHED: *The President Who Almost Lost His Job*

❂❂❂❂❂❂❂❂❂❂❂❂❂❂❂❂❂❂❂❂❂❂❂❂❂❂❂❂❂❂❂❂❂❂

IMPEACHED:

The President Who Almost Lost His Job

❂❂❂❂❂❂❂❂❂❂❂❂❂❂❂❂❂❂❂❂❂❂❂❂❂❂❂❂❂❂❂❂❂❂❂❂❂❂

BY G. ALLEN FOSTER

Illustrated with photographs and prints

CRITERION BOOKS *New York*

Published by Abelard-Schuman Limited

New York   London   An Intext Publisher

❂❂❂❂❂❂❂❂❂❂❂❂❂❂❂❂❂❂❂❂❂❂❂❂❂❂❂❂❂❂❂❂❂❂❂

Re-issued in 1974

Copyright © 1964 by Criterion Books, Inc.

Library of Congress Catalog Card Number: 64-23456

ISBN: 0-200-00139-6

NEW YORK
Abelard-Schuman
Limited
257 Park Avenue So.
10010

LONDON
Abelard-Schuman
Limited
450 Edgware Road W2 1EG

Criterion Books are published by Abelard-Schuman Limited

Published on the same day in Canada by Longman Canada Limited.

Printed in the United States of America

To MARY

CONTENTS

ACKNOWLEDGMENTS

The prints and photographs in this book
are reproduced through the courtesy of:

THE BETTMANN ARCHIVE
   President Lincoln's Funeral in Washington
   Cartoon—*Poor Andy!*
   The Andrew Johnson Impeachment Committee
   The Impeachment of Andrew Johnson
   Thaddeus Stevens being conveyed to the
      House of Representatives
   The Senate as a court of impeachment for
      the trial of Andrew Johnson
   Andrew Johnson

THE NEW YORK PUBLIC LIBRARY
   President Lincoln's Funeral, Springfield, Illinois
   Andrew Johnson and His Wife
   Maj. Gen. U. S. Grant, Gen. W. T. Sherman
   Hon. Gideon Welles, Hon. Salmon P. Chase,
      Hon. Edwin M. Stanton, Hon. Charles Sumner
   Impeachment—The Guard before the War Office
   Cartoon—*King Andy I*
   Scenes from the Impeachment Hearings

ILLUSTRATIONS

IMPEACHED: *The President Who Almost Lost His Job*

FOREWORD

AND BOTH WERE NAMED JOHNSON

*(Written one week, to the hour,
after the funeral of John Fitzgerald Kennedy,
November 25, 1963)*

The drummers stroked the same slow beat on their drums muffled in crepe. The Marine Band sounded the same "ruffles and flourishes" and played *Hail to the Chief*. Both processions started down Pennsylvania Avenue to the mournful strains of Chopin's *Marche Funèbre*. Seven white horses drew the President's body to the Capitol on both occasions. The lone serviceman carried the President's flag behind the body, and the riderless black horse followed. At the Capitol, both martyred Presidents rested on the same black catafalque. At both ceremonies, the former Vice President, now President, stood before the casket—and both were named Johnson.

Abraham Lincoln had been shot in the head with a

President Lincoln's Funeral in Washington

double-barreled Derringer pistol. John Fitzgerald Kennedy died from a head wound delivered by a .25-caliber Italian army rifle. Both men were shot by fanatical enemies of our government.

Lyndon B. Johnson was sworn in at the Dallas Airport within two hours after the death of President Kennedy, on board the President's jet-powered *Air Force #1*. Andrew Johnson was administered the Presidential oath by Chief Justice Chase at ten A.M., April 15, 1865, in the East Room of the White House. President Lincoln had died at seven-thirty A.M. in the little house across the street from Ford's Theater.

On November 26, the day following the funeral of John Fitzgerald Kennedy, President Johnson called a meeting of the Cabinet and asked each Secretary to remain with him. The following day, he went before Congress and stated in no uncertain terms that he intended to carry out the policies of the late President.

Andrew Johnson, immediately after taking the oath, met with the Cabinet, even before Lincoln's body had been brought back to the Executive Mansion. Like the other Johnson, he urged the Cabinet members to remain in office, and he pledged that he would carry out what Lincoln would have done, had he lived. In both cases there were those who didn't like this kind of talk from the new President.

Abraham Lincoln and John F. Kennedy were master political strategists. Lincoln realized that the new Republican Party was a hodge-podge of factions and "isms." Therefore, for his first term he chose as his Vice President a former Free Soil Democrat, Hannibal Hamlin of Maine, and for his second term, a Southern Democrat, Andrew Johnson of Tennessee.

U.S. Senator John Kennedy had observed the programs of Presidents Truman and Eisenhower being hampered by the Republican-Southern Democratic coalition in Congress. Thus, he chose as his Vice-Presidential running mate a Texas senator, and his chief opponent at the Democratic National Convention of 1960, Lyndon B. Johnson.

Some political analysts have already noted that Lyndon Johnson, as a Roosevelt New Deal congressman, was more liberal than John Kennedy as a senator from Massachusetts. Andrew Johnson, somewhat conservative prior to becoming Vice President, suddenly became as liberal as Lincoln. Upon the latter's death, he immediately began fighting for Lincoln's program with the ferocity of a tiger. He was determined to bring the seceded states back into the Union with lightning speed. This he gave top priority.

Even as early as the evening after Lincoln's death, senators and congressmen were swarming around the new President, pledging their support. He should have no concern, they said, they were all with him. Three years later, for accomplishing much that President Lincoln had pledged and died for, Andrew Johnson, the seventeenth President of the United States, became the first and only President of the United States to be impeached by the House of Representatives.

What happened?

It all began with . . .

"With malice toward none; with charity for all; with firmness in the right, as God gives us to see the right, let us strive to finish the work we are in; to bind up the nation's wounds, to care for him who shall have borne the battle, and for his widow, and for his orphan—to do all which may achieve a just and lasting peace among ourselves, and with all nations."

(From the Second Inaugural
Address of President Lincoln)

Then Booth's Derringer led to this . . .

"Are we again prepared to see these fair fields drenched in a brother's blood? Are we not rather prepared to bring from Gilead the balm that has relief and pour it into the wound? They are our brethren, part of ourselves. They are identified with our history, and with all our prosperity. They have lived with us and been part of us from the establishment of the government. . . ."

(From a speech by President Andrew Johnson
in New York City, August, 1866)

Which led to the use of this . . .

"The Senate shall have the sole power to try all impeachments. When sitting for that purpose, they shall be on oath or affirmation. When the President of the United States is tried, the Chief Justice shall preside. And no person shall be convicted without the Concurrence of two-thirds of the members present."

(Article I, Section 6,
The Constitution of the United States)

1 · THE SEEDS OF HATE

House Speaker Schuyler Colfax tapped his gavel lightly on his desk. "The Chair recognizes the gentleman from Ohio."

Representative J. M. Ashley of Ohio, a close friend of Secretary of War Stanton, rose from his seat and stepped to the center aisle of the House, gripping a paper in his hand. With no preliminary speech he read, "I do impeach Andrew Johnson, President of the United States, of high crimes and misdemeanors. I charge him with a usurpation of power and violation of the law: in that he has corruptly used the pardoning power; in that he has corruptly used the veto power; in that he has corruptly disposed of public property of the United States; in that he has corruptly interfered in elections, and committed acts which, in contemplation of the Constitution, are high crimes and misdemeanors."

The House galleries exploded with cheers and applause. After Speaker Colfax had restored order and broken his gavel, the roll was called. The vote to refer the resolution to the Judiciary Committee—that is, bury it—was 108-38.

What had the House done, and *what is impeachment?* By referring Congressman Ashley's resolution to the Judiciary Committee, it was employing a device common in Congress today. It did not want to tell the country that it was not ready to impeach Andrew Johnson at some time. But the impeachment leaders knew they could not rally enough votes at the moment to impeach Johnson decisively. In the Judiciary Committee, the resolution could lie until it died with adjournment, or it could be called up whenever the impeachment leaders were sure of a smashing victory.

Impeachment is as old as the Magna Carta. It is the final legal resort by which the people, through their representatives, may remove a despotic or corrupt government official. During the course of British history, several members of the House of Lords have been impeached. The authors of our Constitution provided for the impeachment of the President and of judges from the Supreme Court down to the federal district courts.

Impeachment is not removal, it is an indictment. In criminal law, a person accused of a felony is brought before a grand jury. There, evidence is produced by the prosecution. If the grand jury finds the evidence impressive, it votes an *indictment*. Having been indicted, the accused must be tried before a jury of his peers which will find either for conviction or acquittal.

Representative Ashley launched the impeachment procedure of the United States when he introduced his resolution. He made the accusation, and it can only be made in the House of Representatives. Had the resolution passed the House, Andrew Johnson would have been impeached on January 7, 1867, instead of in February, 1868.

Having been impeached, the President must stand trial before the United States Senate. The prosecution is a group of "managers" who are lawyer-members of the House. The defense "managers" are selected by the President, but they must not be federal officials. The senators become the jury, presided over by the Chief Justice of the Supreme Court. At the conclusion of the trial, the Senate votes for conviction or acquittal. What happens after that, no one knows. It has never happened.

Had the impeachment supporters been sure of victory that morning in 1867, the resolution would not have been introduced by Representative Ashley. It would have roared from the mouth of their leader, Representative Thaddeus Stevens of Pennsylvania. It has been said that when Thad Stevens entered a room, one could almost smell his hate. He had been hating something or somebody from the Jackson administration until the scene that morning. Now his object of hatred was the South, and anyone who didn't join him in this hatred. There were rumors that Stevens' present hatred was considerably influenced by his mulatto "housekeeper," beautiful Lydia Smith.

This first unsuccessful attempt in the history of the nation to remove a President by impeachment did not begin on that morning of January 7, 1867. It had begun in the second year of Lincoln's administration. Had he not died in that little hall bedroom across the street from Ford's Theater, it is most likely that an attempt to impeach Lincoln would have been made at some point in his second term. Since he was a Republican President with a Republican Congress, it is very unlikely that an impeachment resolution could have passed the House of Representatives. But as early as 1862 there was impeachment talk in the cloakrooms of the House and Senate.

In that year, when Lincoln was rebuffing those who insisted that he emancipate the slaves immediately, a man who was to be the leader in this drama of the nation's first Presidential impeachment rose in the House. Thaddeus Stevens of Pennsylvania thundered at the White House, "The laws of war, not the Constitution, must govern us today. Hang the leaders, crush the South, arm the slaves, confiscate the land. Our generals have a sword in one hand, and shackles in the other. Without a new Cabinet, there is no hope. And what a Cabinet the President has! An assortment of rivals whom he has appointed from courtesy, a stump speaker from Indiana, and *two representatives of the Blair family*." (This was close to a century before the Kennedys came to Washington, but families with several members in the government have always been favorite, and easy, targets for attacks.)

On the morning of December 4, 1865, the Thirty-ninth Congress convened, and Thad Stevens was still thundering. Now he was the acknowledged leader of the Radicals. Radicals—how come? The name had never appeared on a ballot. Officially there were only Republicans and Democrats in Congress. On a straight partisan roll call, the Republicans controlled the House by nearly four to one. Of course, there were no representatives, as yet, from the Southern states.

The Radicals were a hard-core group in the Republican Party that had vehemently opposed Lincoln's plans for a merciful Reconstruction. They believed that the South should be punished. It should be so stripped of its wealth and resources that it could never rise again as a political power. Its people must be punished. The Radicals believed that Southerners had committed treason against their country. These rebels should no longer be considered citizens. Negroes should hold the offices in the Southern state governments. Negroes should hold the seats in the state legislature, guided, of course, by Radical advisors.

The Radicals did not control the Republican majority in Congress. Their strength lay in their unity. Their members took the Radical stand for various reasons, but they clung together in their steadfastness of purpose. Some of the Radicals were sincere idealists. Men such as Charles Sumner and Edward Everett fervently sang Julia Ward Howe's words:

> As He died to make make men holy,
> Let us die to make men free,
> As we go marching on.

They were eager to confer upon the Negro the dignity which he deserved, and they did not trust the South, which had held the Negro in slavery for nearly two hundred and fifty years, to give the Negro equality without federal force.

But the dominant element among the Radicals was a group of aggressive politicians who saw in the Radical movement a chance for what they wanted most—*power*. These men, in the winter of 1865, led by Thaddeus Stevens of Pennsylvania, acted as shrewd strategists. Above all, they knew men. They knew Andrew Johnson, and they knew their fellow Republicans in Congress. They realized that, at the moment, they could not control the Republican majority. So their plan was to jockey the President into a series of situations in which the Republican moderates would have to join them and accept their leadership. To accomplish this, they relied on two factors: Andrew Johnson's innate stubbornness, and the Secretary of War, Edwin M. Stanton, their only friend in the Cabinet.

Outside of the hard-core Radical element, the Republican majorty in Congress represented the many factions which had assembled in 1856 to form a new, liberal party. There were the former Whigs, members of that great national party which had fallen apart from "me-tooism" on slavery. There were the former Know-Nothings, anti-Catholic, and anti-about-everything-else. The former Free Soilers had joined the new Republican Party as had the anti-slavery Democrats from New England. Finally there were the "War Democrats," led by former General John A. Logan, who said they had left their party only temporarily, but who had split with the Southern-sympathizing "Copperhead" Democrats in the Middle West.

With such a hodge-podge of political beliefs gathered under the umbrella of Republicanism, it is not surprising that there was no outstanding party leader. Lincoln had been their leader, but now he was gone, and a Southern

Democrat occupied the White House. The Republicans in Congress, aside from the Radicals, had no definite program. They had followed Lincoln's program, although they didn't agree with all of it. Now they were reluctant to carry out that program and have it administered by a Democrat. They listened to the Radicals when they warned that, should the Southern states be granted full representation in Congress, a Democrat would be elected President in 1868, and the Democrats might control Congress.

The Radicals had one more ace in the hole. Although they were weaker in the Senate than in the House, they had presiding over the Senate as President *pro tempore* their own Ben Wade. Wade, a rough-and-tumble politician from Ohio, had fought his way up the political ladder from Justice of the Peace, District Attorney for Ashtabula County, State Senator, Circuit Judge, to U.S. Senator in 1851.

Under the Presidential Succession Law then in effect, the President *pro tempore* of the Senate succeeded to the White House upon the death or removal of the President. With Ben Wade presiding over the Senate, and actually acting as Vice President, the strategy of the Radicals was clear. It was a logical, step-by-step process. First they would create a series of situations in which the stubborn Johnson must become increasingly distasteful to the Republican majority. When the temper of the majority in both the House and the Senate reached the boiling point, the Radicals in the House would launch impeachment proceedings. With Wade next in line, the Senate would have their choice of convicting Johnson or barring a Republican from the White House. As the Radicals saw it, there could be only one choice. Then with Radical Republican Wade in the Presidency, controlling federal patronage, the Radicals could control the Republican Party and the nation. This was the position of the Radicals at the opening of the Thirty-ninth Congress.

It had not always been thus. Upon Lincoln's assassination, the Radicals welcomed Andrew Johnson with open arms. They had known him in the Senate, just as the senators of 1963 had known Lyndon Johnson. Andy had fought secession there and in his home state of Tennessee. Further, he had made vigorous Union speeches on the stump. Major General Benjamin F. Butler—who later as a congressman from Massachusetts would become one of the most violent Radicals and leader of the prosecution managers at Andrew Johnson's trial—claimed that he talked with Johnson the night after the assassination. Butler reported that Johnson had said, "The rebellion must be subjugated, and the traitors must take back seats." Johnson had said in a recent Illinois speech, "The American people must be taught that treason is a crime, and must be punished." Of this speech, Radical Congressman Julian of Indiana commented, "The President talks like a man on confiscation, and treason."

Now the Radicals were rubbing their hands in glee, convinced that Johnson was one of theirs. The Lincoln Cabinet would go, except perhaps the Secretary of War Stanton who was secretly in their camp. Ben Butler was buttonholing supporters. He wanted to be Secretary of State now, and President in 1868.

Even while Lincoln's body was still lying in an undertaking parlor, and Johnson was presiding over an emergency meeting of Lincoln's Cabinet, the Radicals were waiting to press their program on the new President. As the Cabinet retired, they charged in. Ben Wade assured Johnson, "By the gods, there will be no trouble running the government now."

They all urged Johnson to appoint a new Cabinet. Ben Butler said, "The President must not administer the estate of Lincoln."

The group left the White House elated. The President had been vague, but encouraging. Their jubilee had come and, since Congress was not in session, they either returned to their homes, or put on black crepe armbands and attended Lincoln's funeral in Springfield.

2 · TWO CALLS FROM THE
WHITE HOUSE

Abraham Lincoln was not only a great President, a true humanitarian, and an inexhaustible story-teller. He was a master politician. And if "politician" has become a nasty word, let's say that Lincoln was a peerless political strategist. As the first Republican with a chance of being elected to the Presidency, he was fully aware of the many factions composing the new party which had not yet melded into political unity. Thus, when Thad Stevens described Lincoln's first Cabinet as "an assortment of rivals whom he appointed from courtesy," he was not far from the truth. If Stevens had used "political necessity" instead of "courtesy," he would have hit the bull's eye.

Lincoln was enough of a political analyst to know that the Republicans could not hope to get a majority of the votes in the 1860 election, but he knew that he could win the election if the factions in the Republican Party did not go flying off in all directions as the Democrats had already done. A large wing of the Republican Party had come from the former Free Soil Democrats. Thus, Lincoln insisted that Senator Hannibal Hamlin of Maine be his running mate—Hamlin, who had ridden with Democratic President-elect Franklin Pierce in the 1853 inaugural parade.

Now, in preparing for the 1864 campaign, the need for party unity and a balanced ticket was far more urgent. Lincoln was not even sure of renomination. There was growing sentiment in some quarters to replace him by nominating Treasury Secretary Salmon P. Chase. There were those in Congress who felt strongly that after the succession of Southern victories, and with no immediate prospect of ending the War, Lincoln could not win. Lincoln realized that he could be elected only on a ticket for which all loyal Northerners could vote, and he issued a call for a national convention of what he now called the "Union Party."

If the Union Party were to be all-inclusive, the candidate for Vice President must be a Democrat favorable to prosecuting the War to its end. First, Lincoln considered the man he wanted least, Major General Benjamin F. Butler. Butler had always been controversial and erratic, a lawyer whose ethics some questioned. He had nominated Jefferson Davis for President at the Democratic National Convention of 1860. Now he wanted to hang him. Butler had been such a troublemaker in the Army around Washington that Lincoln had sent him to New Orleans to get him out of the way—and then had had to relieve him of his command. But on the other side of the coin, Lincoln thought, might it not be better to have Butler with him than against him? Ben Butler was a wily politician, a tireless campaigner, and popular with labor.

There was another course, Lincoln decided. How about a dyed-in-the-wool Southern Democrat—one who had fought secession, owned a slave and freed him, a man from a border state who had risked everything he had in maintaining his loyalty to the Union? Lincoln knew such a man. He had been U.S. Senator from Tennessee. At Lincoln's plea he had sacrificed his seat in the Senate to become Provincial Military Governor of his home state. Tennessee was not entirely in Union hands, and for a native son to represent the Lincoln government there was inviting assassination, or at least bodily harm. Lincoln said to himself, "Yes, there is the man—Andy Johnson."

Andrew Johnson and Abraham Lincoln came from the same social background of poverty and ignorance. Both were self-educated. Both had grown to hate slavery, but both believed at the beginning of the War that it was not being fought to free the slaves, but to preserve the Union. This almost identical background had opposite effects on the two men. In Lincoln it produced a kindly tolerance toward all, concern for the poor, pity for the Confederate prisoner, or the Northern deserter—"with charity toward all," as he put it.

In Andrew Johnson his background developed a violent hatred of aristocracy, of oppression in any form, of great wealth in land or money, or of setting class above class. Lincoln could compromise when necessary. Johnson, once he had a cause he believed just, was absolutely immovable. Lincoln's speeches were firm but temperate. Johnson blasted his political enemies with even more vigor than Harry Truman.

Johnson's enemies in Washington whispered about his dubious background. But Johnson's home town of Raleigh, N.C., erected a monument to his father who died when Andrew was four. It seemed that the senior Johnson had died from shock and exposure after he had jumped into an icy river to save two lives.

For a few years the Johnson family was penniless and, as soon as possible, Andrew was apprenticed to a tailor. For one so young, he was learning the trade rapidly and well. But boys of that age have always thrown rocks occasionally. Andrew's aim was poor, and a rock went through a neighbor's window. Terrified lest he might be arrested, he ran away to South Carolina. There he was immediately hired as a tailor's helper. But in Andrew Johnson, honesty was a fierce conviction, and he returned to Raleigh, fully intending to work out his apprenticeship. Upon arrival, he found that the tailor had moved away. Wishing to try his luck elsewhere, Andrew decided on a move to Tennessee. In the meantime, his mother had remarried. One night, Andrew, his mother and the stepfather set out for Greenville, Tennessee, in a rickety cart hauled by a blind pony. At this point, Andrew had never spent a day in school, and was wholly illiterate.

In young manhood, with a well-established tailor shop, Andrew Johnson married. The bride was ambitious for her groom, and immediately undertook to teach him to read and write. Andy was doing well in the tailor shop, and since his skill in reading and writing couldn't keep up with his zest for knowledge, he paid young men seven cents an hour to read to him while he worked at his tailor's bench. Most of the readings were political, and they attracted a forum of hangers-on, usually referred to in the South as "the courthouse crowd." Soon, with Johnson's tailor shop the political discussion center of Greenville, Andrew began to realize that he had a natural talent for debate. To sharpen this aptitude, he frequently made visits to a nearby college where the professors permitted him to challenge the students to debate.

By the time Andrew Johnson was thirty-four, he was comfortably well-off. There were few factory-made clothes before Civil War uniform manufacturers learned mass production methods. Every judge, lawyer, parson, doctor, embalmer, and storekeeper in the Greenville area went to Andy Johnson for his clothes. With this wide acquaintance among influential people, as well as with the carpenters, drovers, shoemakers and farmers, who gathered at his shop to discuss the glory or infamy of Andrew Jackson, Andrew Johnson was now ready for politics. In 1840, he campaigned the state for Van Buren. He found that he was an effective speaker, and he loved campaigning from town to town. He loved the bands and bunting. When the ballots were counted, Johnson was chosen a Presidential elector. At the next election he again hit the campaign trail, and was elected to Congress on the Democratic ticket.

Andrew Johnson's first term in the House of Representatives was undistinguished. Like most freshmen congressmen, he remained silent and voted the party line. But no congressman during that session spent more time in the Library of Congress. Andrew Johnson was determined to be informed. Returning to Tennessee after one term in

Washington, Johnson was elected Governor. In the state capital, he immediately became popular, especially with the working man. Remembering his own illiterate childhood, he pushed through legislation to aid schools and signed a bill, which he had written, establishing a state library. Johnson served one term as Governor and, determined to climb the political ladder, ran for the U.S. Senate and won.

In the Senate, Johnson backed President Franklin Pierce's position that, although slavery was a curse on the nation, it was recognized by the Constitution, and could be abolished only by a Constitutional amendment. He followed Buchanan, but thought him "soft" on the threatened secession of the Southern states.

Senator Andrew Johnson "sat out" the 1860 campaign. Hating slavery, he could not go along with the Breckenridge faction of the Democratic Party. His party loyalty would not permit him to support the moderate Bell-Everett ticket, and he could not bring himself to believe that Stephen Douglas' "squatter sovereignty" theory could work in practice. Not up for re-election that year, Johnson knew that it would be useless for him to campaign extensively in Tennessee for the Democratic Party. Opposed to slavery and secession, he knew that he was politically a "dead duck" in his home state.

Secession and Sumter came as no surprise to Andrew Johnson. He knew the temper of the west Tennesseeans. He had long been convinced that such fire-eating Southern orators as Robert Barnwell Rhett of South Carolina, and editor Roger Pryor of Richmond would whip the South into a fury of rebellion. When war began, Senator Johnson firmly pledged his loyalty to the Union, and to the new

Republican President, Abraham Lincoln. When the Senate convened in July of 1861, Johnson supported all of Lincoln's war legislation. Characteristically, he kept his level head, and was not among those senators who drove out to Bull Run that month, with fine horses and picnic hampers, to watch the Yankees chase the Rebels back to Richmond. Thus he was not among those senators who lashed their horses in a panicky flight back to Washington when it turned out to be the Rebels who did the chasing.

Andrew Johnson had once owned a slave back in Greenville. His conscience had hurt him, and he gave the slave his freedom in a written statement. Johnson then hoped that eventually slavery would be abolished, but not until the answers to many problems could be found, and without seriously and suddenly disrupting the South's economy. He did not believe that states had the moral right to secede. He held with Lincoln that a seceding state was in a state of rebellion, but not legally out of the Union.

Otherwise, Andrew Johnson voted the Democratic platform without the slightest variation. Southerners, who during the difficult Reconstruction era, accused Andrew Johnson of deserting the Democrtaic Party, had forgotten that he had never been anything but a Democrat; that he had not run for the Vice Presidency as a Republican, but as a Democrat on the Union Party ticket. After serving his term as President, Andrew Johnson returned to the U.S. Senate as a Democrat.

One day, half way through Lincoln's first term, Andrew Johnson got a message from the White House. The President wanted to see him, and Johnson could only wonder why. Except on matters of national loyalty, he had voted against Lincoln legislation at every turn. These weren't the old days when he might stop by the White House for a drink of New England rum with President Pierce, or a glass of Monongahela rye with Buchanan. But, personally, Johnson liked Lincoln. They came from the same frontier backgrounds and the same stock. He liked Lincoln's sense of humor, although he had little of it himself.

When Johnson was ushered into the President's office, Abe Lincoln was whistling *The Blue-Tailed Fly* in a sad, subdued tone. He came to the point after a prelude of back-woods stories. A large part of Tennessee had been occupied by federal troops, but not all—and not enough to call a state constitutional convention and organize a loyal state government, as had been done in West Virginia. The state must remain under military rule for some time.

But generals fighting battles had no time to set tax rates, supervise elections, administer state laws, and enforce them. Lincoln asked if Johnson would take the job as Provisional Military Governor of Tennessee.

For Andrew Johnson this was a difficult decision. He loved the Senate, its debate and its camaraderie. His only experience in administration had been his single term as Governor of Tennessee. But there was the other side of the coin. Greenville, Johnson's home town, was in the extreme northeast tip of Tennessee, and was now occupied by federal troops. In this mountainous area, slavery was abhorred—not so much on moral grounds, but because, as on the rocky hill farms of New Hampshire, it was unprofitable. While the rest of the state had gone whole hog for secession, the East Tennesseeans had remained loyal to the Union. They refused to enlist in the Confederate Army.

When drafted, they deserted. Hidden in their mountain coves, they kept up a constant guerrilla warfare against the Confederacy. In return, they were hunted, raided, and hanged by roving troops of Confederate cavalry. As Military Governor, Andrew Johnson could protect his people— so his answer to Lincoln was: "Yes, Mr. President, I'll take the job."

Andrew Johnson's administration of the occupied Tennessee territory was as successful as it could have been under the circumstances. He was hated but respected by the West Tennesseeans. "What could you expect from a renegade like Andy Johnson?" they said. He firmly enforced the laws of the United States, and those laws of the state which did not conflict with the federal Constitution. He was as successful as any man could have been in preventing Yankee soldiers from plundering private property. He did not interfere with slavery where it existed, and he fed the destitute whose lands had been ravaged.

During his tenure as Provisional Governor, Andrew Johnson was often called to Washington. President Lincoln wanted frequent reports on the progress of Reconstruction in Tennessee. As these discussions went on, it was obvious that the President looked upon Johnson's home state as the pilot program for the rebuilding of the whole South after the War. Thus, probably no man in the Lincoln administration knew as much about Lincoln's philosophy of Reconstruction as Andrew Johnson.

Then in the spring of 1864, while Johnson was at the White House giving a report, the President suddenly interrupted him. He wanted his resignation. Johnson was stunned. After all, he had done his best under very difficult circumstances. Then Lincoln gave Johnson his answer. He wanted him as his running mate in November, and he explained his plan for the Union Party.

Johnson protested that he would hurt the ticket rather than help. He said that he feared the President could not be re-elected with a Democrat running with him. Lincoln waved aside this argument. The Republicans would vote for him, and so they would have to vote for Johnson, since there was no way of splitting a Presidential ballot. The loyal Democrats would vote for Johnson, and thus vote for Lincoln. Johnson might even draw some of the Copperhead vote, since a Lincoln-Johnson ticket would assure a just peace for the South. Lincoln said that he was not sure of the nomination, or re-election, but he would feel much more confident with Johnson as a running mate. And Johnson, as he had at the first meeting with the President, said: "I will do it for you, Mr. President."

The Union Party nomination was no push-over for Andrew Johnson, although he ran well ahead on the first ballot at the Union Party National Convention in Baltimore on June 7. The vote on the first ballot was Johnson 200, Daniel Dickinson of New York 108, Hannibal Hamlin of Maine 150, others 59. With Johnson the strongest candidate and obviously Lincoln's choice, most of the delegates switched their votes on the second ballot, and the final tally was Johnson 494, others 59.

Sherman's victories in Georgia, and Grant's in Virginia during the summer and fall of 1864, paved the way for a Union Party landslide in November. The electoral vote

for Lincoln and Johnson, was 212, for McLellan and Pen-
dleton 21. The Democrats carried only New Jersey
and Delaware.

During the winter preceding the inauguration, Vice
President-elect Johnson had many long conferences with
Abraham Lincoln. It was now obvious that the end of the
War was just a matter of weeks. During these conferences,
the President outlined in depth his Reconstruction program.
He first would appoint provisional governors in all of the
seceded states. He would issue a set of standards which a
state must meet before sending representatives to Congress.
New state constitutions must be adopted, conforming to
the federal Constitution. Slavery must be prohibited. The
federal government would take no responsibility for Confederate debts. The states must pledge their allegiance to
the federal Constitution, and must renounce the Confederate States of America should any future action be taken
to reactivate that government.

Then one day when the President seemed to be in a
gloomy mood, he confided in his Vice President-elect: he
hoped he would live to see Reconstruction completed during his second term. He hoped to see every Southern state
represented at the Capitol, and the wounds of war healed.
But he further confided that he had a premonition that he
would not live out his second term. Both he and Mrs.
Lincoln had been dreaming repeatedly of his being shot.

Johnson protested that certainly no Northerner could
wish the President harm, and surely no Southerner who
knew his Reconstruction policy could wish his death.
Lincoln didn't think any Southerner would try to assassinate him unless he were crazy. But Lincoln said he knew

people in Washington who wouldn't shed a tear over his death—Thad Stevens or Ben Butler, for instance. Then the President appealed to Andrew Johnson: if anything should happen to him and Johnson succeeded to the Presidency, he, Abraham Lincoln, would rest easier in his grave if he knew that his Reconstruction policy would be carried out. Andrew Johnson placed his hand over his heart and said, "Mr. President, I swear to God that it will be carried out—to the letter."

Time sped toward Inauguration Day, and to an incident which was to haunt Andrew Johnson for the rest of his life. Andrew Johnson drank moderately in a day when heavy drinking was the rule rather than the exception. It is said that Daniel Webster often consumed a pint of whiskey at breakfast before going to the Senate. There were times when President Franklin Pierce had drunk too much before making public appearances. It had been said of President Buchanan that in the last year of his administration, grieving over the certain break-up of the Union, he used to console himself with large quantities of Monongahela rye whiskey. Grant had been charged with drunkenness, although never in a time of crisis. President Lincoln had said that if he could only find out what kind of whiskey Grant drank, he would prescribe it for the other generals of the Union Army. In the corridors outside the Senate, little old ladies, carrying wicker baskets, peddled wines and brandy to the senators. Not infrequently more than one senator on the floor was intoxicated.

Andrew Johnson sometimes had three or four drinks in the course of a day. At other times he had one, and sometimes he didn't have a drink for a week. There were periods when he drank nothing stronger than sherry. No man had ever seen Andrew Johnson intoxicated. Even his worst enemies testified to that.

Just before the inauguration, Andrew Johnson went back to Greenville to get his wife and daughters, and gather some belongings. The weather was miserable, and Johnson became very ill with a high fever. Three days before the inauguration, he wired Lincoln that he was so ill he could not make the trip to Washington, and asked that the President authorize a federal district judge to administer the Vice Presidential oath in Greenville.

Abraham Lincoln felt guilty in insisting on Johnson's presence on Inauguration Day, but nevertheless he telegraphed Johnson that his appearance was extremely urgent. Grant was in Richmond, and Sherman was chasing General Joe Johnston across North Carolina. The end of the War was only days away. With peace just around the corner, it was imperative that the Vice President, a Southern Democrat, should stand beside Lincoln on the inaugural platform. It would provide a striking symbol of peace and reunion, of Lincoln's Reconstruction.

Andrew Johnson had never let Abraham Lincoln down, and he wouldn't this time. Wrapped in blankets, he "took the cars" and started his strength-taxing trip to Washington. He arrived there the morning before the Inauguration and went straight to his room at the Kirkwood Hotel. That night there was a stag party given by several senators and Cabinet members. Johnson shouldn't have gone, but he did. Everyone was having a wonderful time. Victory was in sight. Every dispatch brought still better news, and the Republicans would be in power for four more years. Everyone was drinking, and Andrew Johnson drank more than was good for a man in his weakened physical condition.

On Inauguration Day, it has always been the custom to administer the oath to the Vice President-elect in the Senate Chamber before swearing in the President. Thus, if the President-elect should die on his ride from the White House to the Capitol, there would be no break in government. On the morning of March 4, 1865, Andrew Johnson rode from the Kirkwood Hotel to "The Hill," and went to Vice President Hamlin's office to rest before taking the oath in the Senate Chamber. Meanwhile, the cavalcade was forming which would escort Abraham Lincoln to the Capitol. Johnson complained that he was feeling ill, but it was an illness induced by a "big night before," commonly known as a "hangover."

The Vice President-elect asked Hamlin for a drink, and the Vice President drew a bottle of brandy from his desk drawer. This he handed to Johnson with a tumbler. Johnson poured the tumbler full and downed it. Even a well man scarcely could have done that and left the room on his two feet. Then, as they waited for the Clerk of the Senate to escort them to the Senate Chamber, the Vice President-elect drank two more brim-fill tumblers while Hamlin looked on in amazement. Next, the Clerk of the Senate entered and announced, "The Honorable Senate is in session, and awaits the Vice President, and the Vice President-elect."

Johnson rose to his feet with no difficulty, and seemed sober when he left the Vice President's office. He was still apparently sober when he reached the Senate Chamber.

But the Chamber was crowded, and the galleries were

full. The inaugural committee, the Republican National Committee, the visiting governors, the Cabinet, the Supreme Court, and the military taxed every inch of space not occupied by the senators. It was cold and raw outside, but in the Senate Chamber it was stifling. Andrew Johnson saw the faces of the senators in front of him begin to blur, and the voice of Vice President Hamlin, calling the Senate to order, was growing faint. President Lincoln, who had just arrived and taken his seat beside Johnson, was alarmed. The Chief Justice came forward to administer the oath, and Johnson didn't seem to realize what was going on. His face was crimson. Meanwhile, the senators were squirming in their seats. Lincoln's face "wore an expression of deep sorrow," to quote a witness. Navy Secretary Welles was whispering to War Secretary Stanton, and shaking his head.

Johnson rose after Hannibal Hamlin had poked him several times and pointed in the direction of Chief Justice Salmon P. Chase. Fortunately, Johnson did not have to walk far; and, fortunately, he knew the Vice Presidential oath, drunk or sober. Albeit, his voice was so thick that he could hardly be understood. At the conclusion of the oath, taken with his hand on the Bible, Johnson stooped unsteadily and kissed the Book. Then he bawled in a raucous frontier voice, "I kiss this Book in the face of my nation of the United States."

There was no unhappier man in the Senate Chamber than Abraham Lincoln. Hearing Radical rumors of Johnson's drinking, he had sent secret investigators to Tennessee for the purpose of checking on Johnson's habits. Their reports were all the same: "Yes, he drinks, but no one has ever seen him drunk."

After the inauguration, Lincoln said to Johnson's critics, "I have known Andy Johnson for many years. He made a bad slip the other day, but you need not be scared. Andy ain't a drunkard."

Nevertheless, at noon on March 4, 1865, Vice President Andrew Johnson *was drunk*, and the Radicals would not soon forget it.

3 · THERE WAS A RIDERLESS BLACK HORSE

It had been a great week in Washington. Lee had surrendered to Grant. A cease-fire was in effect between Sherman and Joe Johnston while negotiations were being conducted, and Washington had never seen such a celebration. It was Friday, April 14, 1865, and President Lincoln was going to celebrate by attending the theater, his favorite form of relaxation. General Grant was at the War Department working on his final report. The President had invited Grant to go to Ford's Theater with him and Mrs. Lincoln. Grant had said that if the report were not finished by the end of the day, he would be happy to accept Lincoln's invitation, but if the report were finished, he would like to catch a train for New Jersey and visit his family.

That Friday, Vice President Andrew Johnson was a man

44

of mixed emotions. Normally not a very religious man, he now thanked God for the coming of peace, and he prayed that it might be Lincoln's peace. At the same time, he could not feel the jubilation of a Northerner. He could not help thinking of the wide swathe of fire and destruction from Atlanta to the sea, and the still-burning plantations in the wake of Sherman's army in North Carolina. He thought of the cities in ruins—Atlanta, Jackson, Columbia, Richmond, Petersburg, and Savannah. It did not make him happy to think of his home state as "The Military District of Tennessee." No, Andrew Johnson did not feel like celebrating, and instead he went to bed early that night of April 14, in his room at the Kirkwood Hotel.

It had been a busy week for Johnson, checking and signing Senate confirmations of Lincoln's appointments—consuls, ambassadors, postmasters, and army commissions. He was tired, and fell asleep as soon as he touched the bed. He didn't know how long he had been asleep when he was awakened by a loud pounding on his door. "What can a Vice President do that anyone should need to wake him in the middle of the night?" he thought, but he arose, pulled a dressing gown over his nightshirt, and opened the door. He faced a sergeant and a squad of soldiers with bayoneted rifles.

"Are you all right, sir?" the sergeant asked.

"Of course, and why shouldn't I be? What's the meaning of all this?" Johnson demanded.

"Are you sure you're all right?" the sergeant repeated, "and has anyone been here?"

"No one has been here," Johnson replied, "and get to the point, man. Why are you here?"

"Well, sir, the President has been shot at Ford's Theater, and he isn't expected to live. Secretary Seward has been stabbed, and there are stories that he is dead. The Secret Service says there is a plot to assassinate you. Secretary Stanton has ordered that the Vice President and all of the Cabinet are to be guarded throughout the night."

Andrew Johnson was speechless. When he found his voice, he asked where the President was lying and demanded to be taken there immediately. The sergeant shook his head. Secretary of War Stanton had ordered that the Vice President not be allowed to leave his hotel. Even under guard there was a danger that an assassin might reach him from a window. To remain imprisoned in his room throughout the night was unthinkable to Johnson, but Stanton was right, and he had to face it. His room contained four easy chairs and a rocker. He offered the easy chairs to the soldiers, so part of the squad could alternate sitting during the night. Then he closed the door, dressed, and carelessly drew the rocker to the window.

In the street outside, an angry mob was already milling about. There were shouts: "Hang Jeff Davis," "Burn the Capitol Prison," "Kill every Rebel in the city," "Hang Johnston and Lee." Slowly Andrew Johnson began to catch the spirit of the mob. His Chief had been shot, and he loved Lincoln as a brother. If the President died, Johnson would take the oath, and wreak vengeance on the South. He would punish every member of the Confederate Cabinet, every general, and every Southern leader.

Then he walked from the window and lit a lamp. On his dressing table was a small autographed photograph of Abraham Lincoln. Johnson picked it up, and tears came to his eyes. As he stared at the picture it seemed to say, "Andy, remember your promise." With his vision blurred by tears, Andrew Johnson returned the picture to the dressing table and nodded. "Yes, Mr. President, I'll carry it out to the letter." Suddenly he felt at peace. He extinguished the lamp and lay down on the bed. He did not awaken until morning.

When Andrew Johnson awoke, he heard the tolling of the bell in the steeple of the New York Avenue Presbyterian Church, the church that Lincoln had attended. The new President dressed and went to the door. The soldiers were still there, and when Johnson stepped into the hallway, they snapped to "*Present*—ARMS!" The sergenat saluted smartly and said, "Mr. President, I have a message for you."

Although the tolling of the church bell had already told Johnson what had happened, the sound of "*Mr. President*" still came as a shock. He took the paper from the sergeant and read: "Chief Justice Chase will be in the East Room of the White House at ten to administer the oath. Signed: Edwin M. Stanton, Secretary of War." Johnson started to put the note in his pocket. Then he looked at it again. This is strange, he thought. Why should Stanton sign the note? Why hadn't it come from Under Secretary of State Freddie Seward, in his father's absence, or from the Chief Justice himself, or from the Attorney General? Why from the Secretary of War?

The soldiers brought Johnson his breakfast, and a newspaper. The newspaper had been printed at eleven P.M., and contained only the barest details of the assassination. Johnson finished the paper, and then for two interminable hours sat in gloomy silence. With every minute he could feel the weight of responsibility crushing down on his shoulders. Many times he had to repeat to himself, "Yes, Mr. President, I'll carry it out—to the letter."

At 9:50 there was a knock on the door. Johnson opened it, and the saluting officer was Colonel Lafayette S. Baker, Provost Marshal of the District of Columbia. The squad of soldiers formed outside the Kirkwood Hotel while Johnson and Baker stepped into a waiting carriage. An escort of cavalry rode with them to the White House where Andrew Johnson went directly to the East Room.

There awaiting him was a sad but impressive assemblage: Chief Justice Salmon P. Chase, the Cabinet, several senators, and friends. Obviously Stanton was running everything. The only Cabinet member absent was Secretary of State Seward. Miraculously he was still alive, unconscious, with a broken jaw, and numerous Bowie knife wounds in his face and throat.

Chief Justice Chase stepped forward solemnly, with a Bible in his hands which he opened. Andrew Johnson placed one hand on the Bible, and raised the other. After the Chief Justice he repeated, "I, Andrew Johnson, do solemnly swear that I will faithfully execute the office of President of the United States, and will to the best of my ability preserve, protect, and defend the Constitution of the United States. So help me God." After he had kissed the Bible, Chase took Johnson by the hand and said, "You are President. May God support, guide, and bless you in your arduous duties." Three years later, Chase was to say, "*Acquitted.*"

After the handshaking was over, and the guests began to leave, President Johnson asked the Cabinet to remain. He told them briefly that he hoped they would all retain their offices, as he wished no changes. He hoped that they would remain with him for the balance of his term. He said there would be no change in the late President's policies, and he asked for their support in the emergency.

The President found that Secretary Stanton had taken over the arrangements for Lincoln's funeral, and he was glad that the sad duty had not fallen on him. However, he was a bit concerned that Stanton seemed to be running *everything*. After a brief conference with Stanton, Johnson went upstairs to offer his sympathy to Mrs. Lincoln, and to tell her that she should remain in the White House as long as she wished. Then the President of the United States, with his guard, rode back to the Kirkwood Hotel.

That night, even before Abraham Lincoln's body had been embalmed, Johnson had a visitor, Senator Charles Sumner of Massachusetts. Sumner, a confirmed Radical, was one of the greatest minds in the Senate. He pleaded with the new President not to be bound by Lincoln's policies, and not to be influenced by the merciful attitudes of Grant, Sherman, and the Blairs. For the most part, Johnson just sat and listened. He didn't trust Sumner. In his opinion, these intellectuals were all fanatics.

The next morning the President dressed for his first full day in office. With the knowledge of a former tailor, and his Jacksonian belief that one did not have to be an aristocrat to be well dressed, Johnson was impeccably turned out. Although born with backwoods features, Andrew Johnson was always immaculately groomed, and his broadcloth frock coats were of the finest quality

Arriving at the White House, Johnson was ushered to

Lincoln's office. The martyred President's unfinished papers were still lying on his desk. Johnson sat down. What to do first? The Vice Presidency of 1865 was not that of Richard Nixon or Lyndon Johnson. The office carried no responsibility or function beyond presiding over the Senate. In spite of the fact that Andrew Johnson had enjoyed a warm personal friendship with Abraham Lincoln, and had conferred with him over policy many times, he still had no knowledge of what really went on at the other end of "The Avenue." And so Johnson sat there behind Lincoln's desk wondering, "How do I start being President?"

Andrew Johnson soon had an answer when Presidential secretary John Hay entered the office. "Mr. President, do you wish me to stay on?" he asked.

"How can I be President if you don't?" Johnson wanted to know. "And what about this business?" he asked, picking up a sheaf of unfinished Lincoln papers on the desk.

"I will explain what they are about," Hay said, "and then you may do as you wish."

"All I wish," replied Johnson, "is to execute them as Abraham Lincoln would have done, had he lived."

By the end of the day, Lincoln's unfinished business had been completed and signed.

Andrew Johnson was a sensitive man, and he felt strongly that no momentous government business should be transacted until after the funeral, which had been set for Wednesday. He had assured the White House staff that they would all be retained. He asked Stanton what part the new President would play at the funeral. Johnson received a polite reply, but between the lines, he could read: "Wait and do as you're told. I'm in charge here."

Johnson received a visit from the Joint Congressional Committee on the Conduct of the War, a committee which had plagued every Union general whose attitude toward the South was short of brutal. They promised their support, and expressed their hope that the South would not get "the milk-sop treatment" promised by Lincoln. "Of course, it was tragic that he should have been shot—but just the same . . ."

During this visit of the hard-core Radicals, the meeting was interrupted by Colonel Lafayette Baker, now heading the hunt for the conspirators who had murdered Lincoln, seriously wounded Seward, and had planned the assassination of Johnson. Azterodt, John Wilkes Booth's accomplice, who had been assigned the job of murdering Johnson, had already been captured, and had confessed his intentions. At the last minute, he had "chickened out."

Now Colonel Baker announced, "Gentlemen, I apologize for interrupting, but this is urgent. We have just received a report that Booth was just seen going into the Kirkwood Hotel. Mr. President, I fear for your safety. May we have permission to search the entire building, including your quarters?" The President of course gave his permission.

While Baker's men were fruitlessly searching the Kirkwood for Lincoln's assassin, Booth was in Virginia. His Washington mistress had taken chloroform, and was very unhappy that the doctors had saved her life.

Between Monday and Wednesday, the day of the funeral, Andrew Johnson had little to do but receive the delegations which were pouring into Washington to mourn the late President and swear the extermination of the South. Stanton, now completely involved in the capture of John

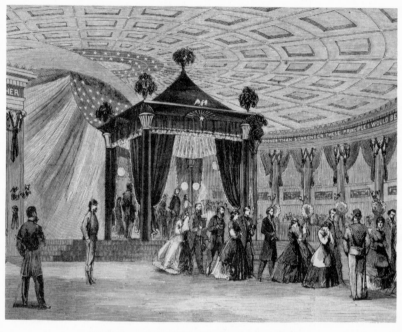

President Lincoln's Funeral—Catafalque
in the City Hall, Springfield, Illinois

Wilkes Booth, had relinquished the funeral arrangements to the Treasury Department. Invitations to the services in the East Room were limited to six hundred.

Wednesday morning finally came. There was an eerie hush over the capital as Andrew Johnson, under heavy guard, rode up Pennsylvania Avenue. As Johnson neared the White House, he passed the military units which would escort Lincoln's body to the funeral train for the ride back to Springfield. Outside the White House, the Marine Band was tuning its instruments softly. The drums were muffled in black crepe.

As the President entered the East Room, the honor guard snapped to "*Present*—ARMS!" The room was already full, and the service was about to begin. The President was escorted to his position by an army major, his sword hilt knotted with crepe. Dr. Gurley, minister of the New York Avenue Presbyterian Church, was standing in the center of the room, before the five-tiered funeral bier on which Lincoln's body rested, and which, ninety-eight years later, would support the body of John Fitzgerald Kennedy. On one side of the casket were the Cabinet, on the other, the Supreme Court. General Ulysses S. Grant stood at the head and President Andrew Johnson took his place at the foot of the casket. The new President nodded to Dr. Gurley, and the service began.

The funeral sermon was mercifully brief. Mary Todd Lincoln, attended by her doctor, was in no condition to bear up long. Like Jacqueline Kennedy, she had sat beside her husband when the bullet pierced his brain. Dr. Gurley, the minister, had been a friend of the former President, and knew Lincoln's love of simplicity. Soon it was over, and the guard of honor bore Lincoln's body to the waiting hearse. Mary Todd Lincoln was virtually carried to her carriage, on which the curtains were drawn. The full-bearded, fatherly Secretary of the Navy, Gideon Welles, went over to Robert "Tad" Lincoln, took the boy's arm, and walked him to the carriage. "Tad" looked into the Secretary's face and asked tearfully, "Mr. Welles, why did they kill my father?"

The ride to the railroad station seemed endless to Andrew Johnson. As he rode behind the Marine Band, and the seven white horses, he wasn't the President. He was just a man mourning for a friend he had loved. The muffled drums stroked out the funeral step. The white horses walked with dignity. Following the body, the riderless black horse, the symbol of a fallen leader since the days of Genghis Khan, pranced nervously. The band played Chopin's *Marche Funèbre*, and the Civil War dirge, *Flee as a Bird to Your Mountain*.

Finally they reached the station. Followed by the Cabinet, Johnson entered the car where Lincoln's body lay, and paid his last respects. Then he returned to the Kirkwood Hotel where he put on an old suit and comfortable walking shoes. He called for a carriage and his Secret Service operative. The pair rode out to Rock Creek where Johnson left the carriage with his guard. Then he walked the trails which relaxed him when he was a senator, and during the period between the election and the inauguration. He walked until dark before returning to his hotel. Now he knew exactly what he would do.

4 · THE FIRST EIGHT MONTHS

With the exception of Franklin D. Roosevelt during the first hundred days of the New Deal, no peacetime President ever accomplished as much as Andrew Johnson did between April and December. It was not until December that Congress convened. Most Presidents have looked forward to those interim periods when Congress is not in session. Those are the periods when they can really get work done without the interruptions of congressional inquiries, time consumed in pushing administration bills through Congress, receiving congressional committees, and preparing long messages to Congress on the budget, and the state of the Union.

Now, left alone with his staff, Andrew Johnson could rush through Lincoln's Reconstruction. If he were successful, he could have all of the Southern states ready for readmission to Congress when that body convened on December fourth. But there were interruptions during that first week of Andrew Johnson's presidency. The first was unexpected, and unpleasant.

Major General Joseph E. Johnston, C.S.A., had offered to surrender his army to General William Tecumseh Sherman, U.S.A. The latter had drafted terms of surrender which he had patterned after Grant's terms to Lee at Appomattox, and according to what he believed Lincoln would have wanted. Both Grant and Sherman, merciless in war, were to prove compassionate in peace. Sherman had sent the surrender terms to Secretary Stanton for the approval of the War Department and the President.

One morning, Stanton charged into the President's office and slammed a sheaf of papers on Johnson's desk. "Sherman should be relieved of his command," he screamed. "Is he trying to outdo Grant? Does he really think those traitors want to take their rifles home just to shoot rabbits? The North won't stand for this."

"I will read the terms and give you my decision," the President replied. Stanton left the room, pulling at his beard.

A few minutes later, Presidential secretary John Hay entered with the newspapers. Johnson picked up yesterday's New York *Times* and stared at the headlines:

STANTON ATTACKS SHERMAN'S

SURRENDER TERMS

In the article, Stanton accused Sherman of opening the way for Jefferson Davis and other Confederate leaders to escape through Mexico to Europe, carrying with them the gold of the Confederacy which they had removed from the banks of Richmond. Stanton concluded his statement with: "They hope, it is said, to make terms with General Sherman, or with some other commander, by which they will be permitted, with their effects, including the gold plunder, to go to Mexico. Johnston's negotiations look to this end." Stanton said that General Grant was being sent to continue operations against Johnston's army.

The *Times* article was backed up by an editorial stating that thousands of Northern lives had been sacrified in vain if Sherman's action represented the attitude of the administration. The South could lick its wounds and start the war all over again. The Northern voters would never forget this outrage.

Andrew Johnson was blind with rage. What right had Stanton to give this statement to the *Times* when he hadn't even showed the terms to the President? His was the responsibility for making a decision on the terms, and here was the *Times* attacking him while the terms were lying in Stanton's desk drawer. And finally, why hadn't Sherman been given a chance to answer Stanton?

Then Johnson put down the *Times* and read the terms. The Confederate Army was to disband, and the regiments were to return to their respective state capitals. The arms and ammunition were to be collected immediately and inventoried. Upon reaching their states, the colonels were authorized to distribute the arms, and permit their men to resume "peaceful pursuits." The people of the former Confederate states were to be guaranteed their "political rights and franchises, as well as their rights of person and property, as defined by the Constitution of the United States, and of the states respectively."

"Not bad," Johnson thought. "Abe would have liked that." But then he gave further study to Sherman's terms. He didn't worry about the distribution of Confederate arms to the men. He didn't believe there was a Confederate soldier who would ever want another taste of war. With farms unworked for four long years, the men would need rifles to supply wild turkey, hare, and deer for their tables.

But this business about the franchise? Wasn't Sherman, a general, going a bit too far in determining the citizenship rights of former Confederates? This would have to take a lot of thinking, and it would have to be done by the Chief Executive. And when Sherman said "the people," did he mean Negroes as well as whites? Johnson knew what Thad Stevens and Ben Wade would say about that. No, the terms would have to be revised, but by Johnson, not Stanton.

The next week was a rip-roaring holiday for everyone in Washington except Andrew Johnson. Thousands watched and cheered as the Grand Review of the Armies marched up Pennsylvania Avenue past the reviewing stand at the White House. There was the Army of the Potomac, Sherman's Army of the Tennessee, and the Army of the West. That week 150,000 men passed Andrew Johnson on the reviewing stand. With them they brought their bands, cannon, horses, supply wagons, and even their beef cattle on the hoof. The President thought that if he heard *When Johnny Comes Marching Home* just once more, he would scream.

On the second day of the review, Sherman led his grizzled Army of the Tennessee up "The Avenue." When the head of the column reached the White House it halted. The leading band struck up *Hail to the Chief*, while Sherman swung his sword up to salute. Then the General dismounted and came up to the reviewing stand. There he was greeted warmly by the President. Sherman, as a good soldier, showed no resentment over Johnson's revision of his surrender terms. But after the greeting, he smartly saluted General Grant, *turning his back abruptly on Secretary Stanton.*

During the week of the Grand Review, Andrew Johnson stood for five hours a day receiving the salutes of the returning veterans. But there was also work to be done, and done under the most difficult circumstances. Outside his office, the line of cigar-smoking, tobacco-chewing hangers-on stretched all the way down the stairs to the sidewalk. Everyone wanted something. Southerners wanted pardons, Union deserters wanted pardons, and the rest wanted political jobs.

In the remaining hours, during which Johnson could concentrate on national problems, he was sending out emissaries to the Southern states to urge these states to adopt new constitutions and reorganize their governments. Louisiana had had its government reorganized as early as 1864. Now Johnson was concentrating on his home state of Tennessee, and it seemed certain that there would be Tennessee representatives in the coming Thirty-ninth Congress.

But Johnson's rapid progress in Reconstruction was being widely reported in the Northern press, and the Radicals were in an uproar. What right had Johnson to be preparing states for readmission with Congress not in session? And what right had Johnson to talk about Southern states? There were no states in the South, they said, there were just conquered territories. They must be punished. They must be ruled by the federal government, and no former Confederate sympathizer should vote. Thad Stevens went one step further: he would let only the Negroes vote, as revenge on their former masters.

The Radicals were now raising an issue which had plagued Abraham Lincoln, and Congress ever since the first Rebel shell burst over Fort Sumter: *What was the Confederacy?*

In 1861, after the provisional government of the Confederate States of America had been formed at Montgomery, Alabama, the new government sent a team of commissioners to Washington. Their assignment was to prepare for the settlement of many problems essential to the peaceful division of the North and South. How about mail service between the two nations? What would be the procedure for the Confederacy taking over the Southern forts of the U.S. Army? Southern taxes had helped build them, along with the forts in the North, so there should be no question of the Confederacy's right to take them, the South believed. What about import and export duties between the two countries, and navigation on the Mississippi River?

When the commissioners reached Washington, Lincoln refused to see them, and then referred them to Secretary of State Seward. Why he had anyone see the commissioners is a mystery in the light of his soon-disclosed policy. The commissioners were confused. To them, being received by the Secretary of State was recognition of the Confederacy. Seward heard their proposals and said he would discuss them with the President. When the commissioners returned, they received only vague comments from Seward, the suave New York politician. After a week of double-talk by Seward, the disillusioned and angered commissioners returned to Montgomery. The Confederacy began arming.

Lincoln's rebuff of the Confederate commissioners was extremely important in his long-range planning. If he refused to recognize the C.S.A. as a nation, and considered the eleven seceded states as simply in rebellion, they would still be states at the end of the War. They would have stable state governments, and their representatives could return to Congress as soon as the states had ratified any amendments to the Constitution which had become law in the meantime.

But after the War had begun, the Radicals took a view opposite to Lincoln's. They believed Lincoln was unrealistic. There was an established government, the Confederate States of America. It had a constitution, a Congress, a President with a Cabinet, and a judicial system. It collected taxes as a federal government. The Confederate Army and Navy fought under a Commander-in-Chief, not under the governors of eleven seceded states.

The Radicals, like Lincoln, were convinced that the North would win the War. But they said the victory would be over the Confederate States of America, not over eleven seceded states in rebellion. Those states had ceased to exist as part of the Union after they had seceded and ratified the Confederate Constitution. With defeat, the states would only be conquered territories to be occupied and ruled. Their citizens would be defeated traitors, and treated as such. If anyone should rule, it should be the Negro.

Now a very knotty problem faced Andrew Johnson which temporarily diverted his attention from Reconstruction. Confederate President Jefferson Davis had been captured, and was in prison at Fortress Monroe, Virginia. What to do with him? The Radicals screamed for a military trial, and hanging. Johnson balked at that. No military trial at the time could possibly be fair, and besides, Davis was a civilian. Johnson thought he should be tried in a federal district court, but there were no federal courts in Virginia in the summer of '65, and if there were, what Virginia jury would ever convict Jefferson Davis? Johnson suggested to Chief Justice Salmon P. Chase that the former Confederate President be tried by the Supreme Court, but Chase objected. In the first place, Davis should be tried at the place of his alleged crime, Richmond. Secondly, Chase ruled that the Supreme Court could not sit as a trial court outside the District of Columbia.

Johnson had always hoped that Davis would escape from the country. Both Grant and Sherman expressed similar hopes in their memoirs. But Davis was in prison, a sick old man, bitter both over defeat and over the lack of support the Confederate Congress had given him. There were reports, and they were true, that Davis was being mistreated. A light was kept burning in his cell all night, and a guard with a cocked rifle stood over him at all times. He was in chains. For an old man, who had suffered most of

Andrew Johnson and His Wife

his life from neuralgia of the eyeballs, this treatment was torture.

When the reports reached Johnson, he was furious. Although unpopular, Jefferson Davis was a great symbol to the South. His mistreatment could harm the atmosphere of Reconstruction. The President told Chief Justice Chase to have Davis released on bail—how, he didn't care.

Throughout the summer and fall, every news dispatch from Washington fanned the flames of Radicalism. Jeff Davis had not been hanged! Lee had not been punished, and he had been permitted to become president of Washington College in Virginia. There he would indoctrinate another generation of Southern youth in secession, they said. With Southerners voting again, the Republican Party would be destroyed. And why weren't the Negroes voting, they asked? Johnson was doing nothing to punish the South. He wants the South in his control, they charged. Just wait until the next session of Congress!

Then came Thanksgiving Day. As Andrew Johnson carved the turkey for his sickly wife and two charming daughters, he was truly thankful. Every Southern state except Texas was ready for readmission. His home state of Tennessee had qualified for representation in the next Congress, and had elected a congressman from one district. Johnson would make a trip there soon—as President instead of "the East Tennessee renegade." Yes, when the Tennessee boys came to Washington, he would hold a White House reception, he thought. But he thought wrong.

5 · THE TOOL

In the early summer of 1865, everyone agreed that *something* must be done about the suddenly-freed Negro. At one extreme were the white Southerners who feared a black insurrection. Immediately, in panic, the Southern states began passing Black Codes. These laws defined the status of the Negro. He could own property, sue or be sued, he must live in segregated districts, and he must not leave a job without the permission of his employer, or the police. Any Negro found idle was to be put in jail. Negro preachers, who were wandering through the South, calling for the blacks to assert their equality, were locked up as vagrants.

At the other extreme were the Radicals, including both intellectual idealists and power-seeking politicians. The

Radicals demanded that the blacks be given the vote immediately. They wanted the large plantations to be broken up, and the land given to Negroes for small farms. They insisted that the Southern whites be suppressed to the extent that the Negro vote would control every Southern state. This, they thought, would keep the Republican Party in control for at least a generation.

The leader of the idealists was the Harvard-educated, intellectual, Senator Charles Sumner of Massachusetts. He maintained that the Negro was the intellectual equal of the white, and was immediately qualified to vote. The political bosses of the Radicals were Senator Ben Wade of Ohio, now President *pro tempore* of the Senate, and Representatives Thad Stevens and Ben Butler. Both Wade and Butler had Presidential ambitions, and wanted the Southern Negro vote.

Then there were the middle-of-the-roaders, who believed that the Negro needed, in this order: jobs, education, *and then the vote*. This group included all of the Democrats in the House and Senate, and the moderate Republicans.

On one point these three factions were in agreement: a government agency must be created to provide for the welfare of the Negro. He must be fed until jobs were available, schools must be established, and the Negroes must be encouraged to settle down in their communities, and cease wandering aimlessly from town to town. The question was, who was to control the agency? President Johnson naturally believed that the agency should be a branch of his executive department, perhaps under the Army. The Radicals wanted it responsible to Congress. The agency could control the Negro vote.

To understand the condition of the blacks in 1865, it is necessary to go back thirty-four years to 1831, for since that year, the status of the Negro had deteriorated. Before 1831, many Negroes had been educated to some extent. Plantation owners sometimes supported Negro schools. Some slaves became so skilled in arithmetic that they kept their masters' account books. The wives of plantation owners often conducted Sunday School classes for the children of slaves, and taught them to read the Bible. Then in 1831 came the Nat Turner slave insurrection. Raging through Virginia, this uprising took the lives of many whites and blacks before Turner was captured and executed.

Immediately the Southern state legislatures began passing laws prohibiting the education of Negroes, especially in reading and writing. Then when copies of *Uncle Tom's Cabin* and Abolitionist pamphlets began infiltrating the South, more laws were passed making it a punishable offense for a Negro to be found with any kind of printed material. Therefore, in 1865, through no fault of their own, most Negroes were wholly illiterate.

With Lee's surrender, the Negro became a confused, bewildered member of American society. The "social security" of slavery was over. The first reaction of many Negroes was that freedom from slavery meant freedom from work. They left the plantations and congregated in the villages to sing, dance, loaf, or just mill around. But soon they were hungry, and no one fed them. Now they could only eat with money in their pockets, and the man with five children had to have more money than the man with two. Often there were aged, crippled parents to support. The plantation owners had always taken care of the old folks.

It was not that there was no work for the freed Negroes to do. There was more work to be done than ever before. Ruined cities, railroads, and burned plantation buildings must be rebuilt, and food must be grown. But there was no money. The banks were bursting with currency, but all of the dollar bills bore the portrait of Jefferson Davis— absolutely worthless.

Many of the Negroes passed from involuntary servitude to voluntary servitude. They went back to their old owners and worked for nothing, just to eat. Some plantation owners gave some of their former slaves small parcels of land, enough for a cabin, and a little garden. It reduced the owners' taxes. On other plantations, sharecropping, which still haunts the South, began. But for the vast majority of Negroes there was nothing to do but line up in front of the U.S. commissary depots for hand-outs.

Then the first wave of "carpetbaggers" moved in. They were Northerners who got their name from the fact that they arrived in the South with no more belongings than could be packed in a carpet bag—a bag made of carpeting, little larger than a modern overnight case. They were pure opportunists and adventurers. They knew that they could buy anything they wanted, *at their price*, with sound U.S. currency, and sell later at huge profits. They knew that there would be a vast number of federal jobs while the South was under military rule. If they couldn't get federal jobs, they would run for public office and be elected by Negro votes, votes bought with a barrel of flour.

Meanwhile the Negroes were being confused by wild

Hon. Gideon Welles

Hon. Salmon P. Chase

Hon. Edwin M. Stanton

Hon. Charles Sumner

tales from the North. Chief Justice Chase had gone on a
pointless junket through the South, promising all kinds
of good things for Negroes and repentant whites. Up in
Washington, Thad Stevens was promising every male Negro "forty acres and a mule." All of the Negroes were to
vote, but not the whites.

Yes, everyone agreed that there should be an agency to
look after Negro welfare. Probably Andrew Johnson
should have made the first move, but the man in the White
House was completely bogged down in administrative
detail. He was working himself into illness. In this day of
Civil Service examinations, it is difficult to imagine the
patronage problem of Andrew Johnson's administration.
Even Franklin Pierce, in 1852, had 30,000 government jobs
to fill by personal appointment.

And so it was the Radical faction of Congress which
pushed through the bill creating the Freedmen's Bureau.
On its face, the Freedmen's Bureau was machinery of com-
passion. It turned out to be, in some respects, a political
monstrosity. Johnson, not envisioning what was to happen,
signed the bill.

The Freedmen's Bureau was first placed under the Army,
with Major General O. O. Howard in command. The
General divided the South into ten Bureau districts with
a commissioner in charge of each. The objectives of the
Bureau would seem even beyond the range of today's "big
government"—to make as rapidly as possible a general
survey of conditions and needs in every state and locality;
to relieve immediate hunger and distress; to appoint state
commissioners and upwards of nine hundred bureau officials; to put laborers to work at regular wages; to transport

laborers, teachers, and officials; to furnish land for the Negroes to establish hospitals and health stations; to administer justice between man and former master; to answer continuous criticism, North and South, black and white; *to find funds to pay for all this.*

No bureau was ever created with a nobler purpose, or with a greater invitation to corruption. The first operations of the Freedmen's Bureau were heartening to all, especially the blacks. Soon schools were opening, local bureaus were serving as employment agencies, local commissioners were supervising labor contracts and setting wages. The needy were being fed, and the sick healed. Many Negro children were receiving better education than the children of whites. In Virginia, General Samuel Armstrong founded Hampton Institute, now an outstanding college for Negroes, and Hampton served as a model for such fine schools as Tuskegee.

But where could over nine hundred competent, honest officials be found to administer a program which would stagger our present-day Department of Health, Education, and Welfare? There were no trained social workers in 1865. Competent officials were not found in sufficient numbers, and soon it was evident to Andrew Johnson that the Freedmen's Bureau was becoming a huge political grab-bag. The carpetbaggers, backed by the Radicals, were having a field day. Bureau supplies were being misappropriated and sold to whites at high prices. The money went into many officials' pockets. General Howard could not believe the tales of corruption in the Bureau, but Andrew Johnson was convinced that they were true.

In February, 1866, the law which created the Freedmen's

Bureau and appropriated its funds was about to expire, and Senator Trumbull of Connecticut introduced a new bill. It was much like the first, but it contained new provisions giving the commissioners powers unheard of in peace time —powers to arrest, try, and sentence whites for any violations of Negro civil rights. Today, persons may be arrested by a U.S. marshal for violations of any existing civil rights legislation, but the arrested are tried in federal courts before a judge, and they are entitled to defense counsel. Under the Trumbull Bill, a Southern white could be hauled before a carpetbag commissioner, who had never seen a law book, and convicted without a defense counsel or a jury.

The Trumbull Bill was passed by both houses of Congress, and went to the White House where Andrew Johnson was waiting for it, knowing what he must do. He promptly vetoed the bill. His veto message to Congress was firm but moderate in tone. He praised the great humanitarian accomplishments of the Freedmen's Bureau. He desired its continuance, but he could not sign a bill which gave to other than the Justice Department the authority to enforce the law. It was absolutely unconstitutional, he said. Of course, the President could have signed the bill and let the Supreme Court rule on its constitutionality. But Andrew Johnson wasn't that kind of a man.

After listening to Johnson's veto message, the first on a Radical-supported bill, Congress promptly passed the bill over his veto. Now the whispers of "impeachment" were becoming shouts.

6 · THE SOUTH DIDN'T HELP MUCH

Just at the time when Andrew Johnson was trying to demonstrate that Lincoln's Reconstruction could be both successful and just, the white South was not doing much to improve its image.

The night before the Thirty-ninth Congress convened, a group of young Confederate veterans were sitting beside the fireplace in a lawyer's office in Pulaski, Tennessee. They were fun-loving, bored, unemployed, and looking for some deviltry. Someone suggested forming a secret society, with solemn oaths, a ritual, and some kind of costume—just for the heck of it. The lodge would be extremely secret, and no one would know who belonged to it. For utmost secrecy, they would never meet at the same place, and they would ride masked to and from meetings—

great idea! Then someone suggested that wearing bedsheets, with eyeholes cut out, would not only mask the
members, but also make them look spooky. "Now you've
hit the target, brother!"

At the next meeting, John Reed, who knew a smattering
of Greek, came up with a suggested title: "Kuklos, meaning "circle." The group liked the idea, but one member
suggested splitting it into two words—Ku Klux. And then
a boy of Scotch descent added "Klan." Thereupon, someone found some red paint and printed "K K K" on the
bedsheets. The Ku Klux Klan was born.

Now the "circle" of ex-Rebs was bursting with deviltry.
A voice from under a sheet said, "Come on, let's ride out
and see if we can put a little life in old Pulaski." Immediately they were on their horses, galloping down the road,
and whooping the Rebel yell. The first place they passed
was a Negro shack, the family sitting on the front porch.
When the Negroes saw the hooded riders in the eerie
moonlight, they screamed and dashed for the woods. As
they rode along, other Negroes, and some whites, retreated
speedily. The Klansmen laughed. It was a great joke. That
their Ku Klux Klan would become a great instrument of
terror to the Southern Negro not once entered their hell-
raising heads.

For some time, the Pulaski Ku Klux Klan continued as
a purely, fun-loving, social organization. The boys were
having so much fun they gradually began to let in other
young veterans from nearby communities. Their night-
riding, except for the fright it gave some superstitious
blacks, was as harmless as tricks-or-treats on Hallowe'en.
The Klansmen reveled in their new awesome ritual, their

fiery crosses, and their titles: Imperial Wizard, Grand
Cyclops, Kleagle, Grand Magi, Grand Turk, etc.

But watching the effectiveness of the Pulaski Klansmen
in scaring blacks were men who had other ideas of what
could be done behind the anonymity of a white bedsheet.
They sought admittance to the Klan, and began founding
Klaverns—lodges—in their home towns. Once outside the
borders of sleepy Pulaski, the Klan spread like a cancer.

Now there were dues, and regalia to purchase. The latter
was becoming more elaborate. The bedsheet was now a
shoulder-to-ankle robe. The hood was a separate piece
containing a skullcap from which protruded a tall white
spike. Some of the officers' regalia were of different colors,
denoting rank. The horses were robed and hooded with a
spike protruding from the head-piece, making the horse
look like the legendary unicorn. This was practical. In
most Southern communities a man could be identified as
well by his horse as by his face.

At first, the now widespread Klan confined itself to
scaring Negroes into "keeping their place." Then it progressed to reading blood-curdling warnings to "uppity"
Negroes. But it was not long before the now elaborate
robes were concealing holstered Colt revolvers. Negro
cabins were burned, and the occupants were chased off
their land. There were hangings, and murder by torture.
The blacks naturally ran to the U.S. Army officers or to
the carpetbaggers running their Freedmen's Bureau. The
word went back to Washington, and into the Northern
press. Thad Stevens rubbed his hands in glee—"Andy Johnson, you're responsible for this, and you couldn't have done
more for our side. *You and your merciful peace.*"

New Orleans had suffered longest from the War. Since
1862 the city had been occupied by federal troops, and
under military rule. The people had lived through a year
of Ben Butler's vengeful tyranny and corruption. Then
there had been General Banks, almost as bad. Finally there
was Sheridan. Sheridan, like Sherman, had been for shorten-
ing the War by devastation. But with peace, Sherman urged
a speedy and merciful reconciliation with the South, while
Sheridan administered the military occupation of New
Orleans as though Thad Stevens were Secretary of War.

But in spite of all that Louisiana had suffered, its people
had met Lincoln's standards for readmission to the Union
as early as 1864. The state had adopted a new constitution,
and fully expected to send representatives to Congress. The
new constitution met with Andrew Johnson's approval,
but it was distasteful to the Radicals. The Negro was not
yet enfranchised (but neither was he voting in Ohio, New
Jersey, Minnesota, or Kansas).

With guidance from the Radicals in Congress, the New
Orleans carpetbaggers called for a new constitutional convention. The constitution then in effect stated that a new
convention could be called only by the chairman of the
previous convention, Judge Edward H. Durell. The Judge
saw no need for a new constitution, since Lincoln and
Johnson had both approved the present document. Then
Governor Madison Wells, who had been elected with
Radical support, went over Durell's head and ordered a
convention to convene in New Orleans on June 26, 1866.
With some 150,000 Louisiana voters disenfranchised because of some form of support for the Confederacy, the

Radicals were able to elect a full slate of delegates, including some Negroes.

As the delegates began to gather in New Orleans, the temporary state capital, there also arrived a horde of Confederate veterans, and their sympathizers from all over Louisiana. Most of them were armed with revolvers or knives, and were prepared to dissolve what they considered an illegal convention. That there would be trouble was obvious to all. At this moment, Governor Wells found it convenient to have business in the northern part of the state, and left the city. At the same time, General Phil Sheridan, commander of the Military District of Louisiana, decided there were matters in Texas which required his attention. Left to face the crisis in New Orleans were Mayor Monroe and General Absalom Baird, second in command to Sheridan. Baird's troops were stationed at Jackson Barracks, several miles from downtown New Orleans.

Both Baird and Monroe were uneasy. Mayor Monroe, scion of an old New Orleans family which retains its prominence today, knew well the temper of the crowd which had mobilized to block the convention. Baird, whose military record is obscure, did not know where to find Sheridan, and telegraphed to Secretary of War Stanton for instructions. But no instructions came. With no word from the War Department, Baird ordered his troops to remain at Jackson Barracks until the hour of the constitutional convention. Intentionally, or erroneously, Baird said that the convention would meet at six P.M. The hour of the convention had been set for noon.

While Mayor Monroe was issuing his proclamation calling for peace and order during the convention, and General Baird was making his "preparations" to prevent disorder, a series of mass meetings were being held by the Radicals, the former Rebels, and the blacks. At every meeting fire-eating orators were doing their best to stir passions of hate.

Among the worst of these was a recently arrived Yankee dentist, Dr. A. P. Dostie. At a Negro mass meeting, he said in part, "On Monday I want you to come into your power . . . I want only brave men to come who will stand by us . . . We have three hundred thousand black men with white hearts. Also one hundred thousand good and true Union men . . . Sheriff Harry Hayes, with his posse may be expected here, and the police, with more than a thousand men sworn in, may interfere with the convention . . . but if we are interfered with, the streets of New Orleans will run with blood. . . ."

The Negroes weren't interested in blood, they just wanted citizenship.

The convention which had been called for July 26, didn't get under way until the thirtieth. The delegates convened at noon, but it was found that a quorum was lacking, and the convention adjourned until one P.M. In the meantime, a peaceful demonstration of Negroes was forming just off Canal Street. Its purpose was simply to demonstrate that the black population of the city was solidly behind the convention in its determination to enfranchise the Negro population of Louisiana.

The orderly parade, headed by an American flag, and a band, moved up Canal Street. It met no opposition until it reached the intersection of St. Charles. There its way was blocked by a large crowd of sullen whites. The Negro procession doggedly began to push its way through. There were a few scuffles, and someone fired a revolver. But at that moment, a wave of regular and auxiliary police arrived and restored order. It looked as though the crisis was over. Then for some unknown reason, a police officer grabbed a white newsboy. Somebody, none knew on which side, shot the policeman. It was all that was needed. All hell broke loose in a second. The white mob, heavily armed, drove the blacks to the convention hall where they took refuge. Now the police joined the mob in surrounding the convention hall and storming it. Both blacks and whites were dragged from the hall and butchered.

When General Baird's troops arrived at 2:40, it was all over, but in one hour and forty minutes, at least two hundred Negroes had been killed. Mayor Monroe later announced that forty-two policemen had been killed or wounded. There was no record of the white civilian casualties.

The New Orleans massacre was all the Radicals in Congress had been waiting for. It was proof, they said, that loyal men were not safe in the South. They said the riot provided proof that the South must be punished by continuing to remain under military rule, and they blamed the whole affair on the Democratic Party, the party of Andrew Johnson. In the Senate, Oliver P. Morton shouted, "Every unregenerate Rebel calls himself a Democrat, every sneak who ran away from the draft calls himself a Democrat. Every man who murdered Union prisoners, who invented hellish compounds to burn steamboats and Northern

cities, calls himself a Democrat. . . . In short, the Democratic Party may be described as a common sewer and a
loathsome receptacle."

Andrew Johnson was puzzled by the New Orleans
affair. He could understand the temper of the New Orleans
population. It had been persecuted by one military ruler
after another, and Sheridan had been the last straw. Something had to give sooner or later. But why hadn't Sheridan
acted sooner? He could have prevented the illegal convention from meeting. He could have policed the streets
of the city. And why had he gone to Texas when he knew
a dangerous crisis was in the offing? Had anyone told
Sheridan to go to Texas? "Quite possibly," Johnson
thought.

While the Radicals in Congress were busy enacting new
abominations against the South, President Johnson set a
course later followed by Presidents Wilson, Roosevelt,
Truman, and Eisenhower. He set out on a tour of the
North, carrying the Lincoln-Johnson Reconstruction program to the people. For window-dressing, he took along
two heroes, General Grant and Admiral Farragut, plus
several Cabinet members. The tour started successfully,
and Johnson received warm receptions from the Democrats
of New Jersey, Maryland, and New York City. Traveling
through upstate New York, he was well received by large
crowds, but as he approached the Mid-West, it was noticeable that organized heckling was on the increase. The local
politicians evidently had been "given the word" from
Washington.

One of Andrew Johnson's regrettable weaknesses was
his inability to handle hecklers. It is an unforgivable weak-

"POOR ANDY!"

Cartoon—*Poor Andy!*

ness in a politician. Instead of ignoring the hecklers, or making them look ridiculous by a well-turned wisecrack, Andrew Johnson lost his temper and fought back.

His first blast came in Cleveland, Ohio. Someone asked him why he wasn't doing something about Negro suffrage. Johnson flushed and shouted back, "Let the Negroes vote in Ohio before you talk about Negroes voting in Louisiana. . . . You are very much disturbed about New Orleans, but you won't let a Negro go to the ballot box in Ohio." What the President said was true, but it wasn't the kind of an answer an audience expects from a President. And this was but the first in a series of similar Presidential outbursts.

During a speech in St. Louis, he answered a heckler with: "I have been called a Judas Iscariot. There was a Judas once, one of the twelve Apostles. The twelve Apostles had a Christ, and he could not have had a Judas unless he had had twelve Apostles. If I have played the Judas, who has been my Christ that I have played Judas with? Was it Thad Stevens? Was it Wendell Phillips? Was it Charles Sumner?"

Andrew Johnson may have forgotten these words as soon as they were uttered, but newspaper reporters recorded them, and Johnson was to recall them when they were entered as evidence at the impeachment trial.

The President's next move was to call a Union Party National Convention in Philadelphia. This was not to nominate a candidate for President, but an attempt to renew the national unity which Lincoln achieved through his coalition of Republicans and loyal Democrats. It would again highlight the fact that Johnson was carrying on for Lincoln.

The convention turned out to be a brilliant piece of public relations on Johnson's part. Meeting on August 14, 1866, the convention opened on a happy note with the leadership shared by the Republicans and Democrats. Northern and Southern Democrats joined hands for the first time since the election of 1860. Delegates had the heart-warming sight of a Confederate and a Union officer marching down the center aisle, arm in arm. The delegates unanimously denounced slavery, and voted for "equal protection and every right to personal property for the Negro." There were glowing tributes to Lincoln, and high praise for Johnson.

At the conclusion of the convention, a committee of delegates was sent to call upon Andrew Johnson at the White House and express the convention's approval of his administration. Here again, Johnson unfortunately let his tongue get out of control. First, he thanked the committee for its support, and told the members that the speeches at the convention would have a profound effect on public opinion. He should have stopped right there. The convention had received a good press, and the speeches were having a marked effect.

But then Andrew Johnson let off a blistering blast at the Radicals. "We have seen Congress organized," he said, "we have seen how Congress in its advance, step by step, has gradually been encroaching upon constitutional rights and violating the fundamental principles of government, day after day, and month after month. . . . With the bill called the Freedmen's Bureau, and the army placed at my discretion, [laughter and applause] I could have remained at the capital with fifty or sixty millions of appropriations, with the machinery to be worked by my own hands, with my satraps and dependents in every township in the United States, and all the patronage of the government, I could have proclaimed myself a dictator [laughter—'That's right']. My pride and my power is, if I have any, to occupy that position which leaves the power in the hands of the people [applause]. It is upon them that I have always relied; it is upon them I now rely ['And they will not desert you'—applause].

Andrew Johnson's speech to the delegates was widely publicized, but the Radical press failed to include the laughter, making it appear that Johnson was serious when he said that he could be a dictator. The Radicals in Congress twisted his allusions to the army and the people to mean that Johnson was trying to gain popular support to drive Congress out of the Capitol by military force. Again, Andrew Johnson was to read his words in the official transcript of the impeachment trial.

7 · THE FIGHTING THIRTY-NINTH

In the 1920 Presidential campaign, Warren G. Harding defeated his Democratic opponent, James M. Cox by running on a platform of "Back to Normalcy." The American people of that year were tired of wartime restrictions and strong government. The people of 1866 were in the same mood. Andrew Johnson succeeded a man who had assumed more executive power than any resident of the White House in our history. It has been said that not even Wilson, Franklin Roosevelt, or Truman exercised such emergency wartime powers without authorization from Congress as gentle, kindly Abraham Lincoln. He called out an army of 75,000 while Congress was not in session. He fought the Battle of Bull Run without a declaration of war. Later he suspended the constitutional right of *habeas corpus* in districts which were not in rebellion. When the Southern-sympathizing Knights of the Golden Circle became active in Ohio, Lincoln declared the state a military district and placed General Burnside in command. When the Thirty-ninth Congress convened on January 7, 1867, the mood of the Republican majority in both the House and the Senate was to cut back the authority of the chief executive to where it had been before the Civil War. Taking advantage of this mood, the Radicals were able to woo the more moderate Republicans by shouting "Dictator!" at every executive act of Andrew Johnson. With this strategy the Radicals had grasped the leadership in both houses of Congress, and their supreme potentate was Thaddeus Stevens of Pennsylvania.

Crippled from birth by a deformed foot, and born in poverty, Stevens seems to have borne a grudge against society. From his first election to the state legislature, and through his many terms in the House of Representatives, he was always fighting something or somebody. He was always against, never for. Now at the opening of the Thirty-ninth Congress, Thad Stevens was an old man— feeble but fiery.

Evidence of what was to be the strategy of the House Radicals in this session of Congress was seen even before Schuyler Colfax of Indiana was elected Speaker and the House organized. The Clerk opened the session by calling the House to order, and proceeded to call the roll of states. By some tradition, so old that no one could remember its purpose, the roll was not called in alphabetical order, but started with Maine. Sitting on the Democratic side of the aisle was a stranger to the House. He was Horace Maynard.

Throughout the War he had remained loyal to the Union, and had even made army recruiting speeches in New York. Now under the Lincoln-Johnson Reconstruction program, with which Tennessee had fully complied, Maynard had been duly elected to Congress. He eagerly waited for the Clerk to call "TENNESSEE," and he wished that Andrew Johnson could be there to hear him answer. Then the next state to be called should have been Tennessee, but the Clerk called "INDIANA."

Maynard immediately rose to be recognized, but the Clerk ruled that no representative would be recognized until the completion of the roll call. When the roll of the states was completed, Maynard rose again. Now the Clerk said that he would not recognize any member until a Speaker had been elected. The election of Schuyler Colfax took but a few minutes, and the new Speaker took over the gavel. Again Maynard asked for recognition. Colfax said he could not recognize anyone who was not a member of the House, and Maynard's credentials had not as yet been accepted.

Now Congressman James Brooks of New York City, a Democrat and a newspaper editor, joined the fray. He demanded to know how, if the House considered that Tennessee was not in the Union, could Andrew Johnson sit in the White House? Colfax ruled Brooks out of order, inspiring a rousing cheer from the Radicals. In a dramatic half hour the House had revealed its attitude toward admitting representatives from the states which had complied with President Johnson's Reconstruction standards. The work of Johnson's year and a half in office was now stymied.

To make no mistake about this Thad Stevens now took the floor and introduced this resolution: "Resolved, by the Senate and the House of Representatives . . . that a joint committee of fifteen members shall be appointed . . . who shall inquire into the condition of the states which formed the so-called Confederate States of America, and report whether they or any of them are entitled to be represented in either house of Congress . . . and until such report shall have been received, and finally acted upon by Congress, no member shall be received into either house from any of the said so-called Confederate States of America. . . ."

The vote on the resolution was: For, 138; Against, 36. All the years of planning and working by Lincoln and Johnson had gone for naught—by a four-to-one vote. Stevens was overjoyed. Now his new Reconstruction Committee would run the show, and Andy Johnson would be stripped of his power. By keeping the Southern states out of Congress, the Radical Republicans would be in power until a Republican President could be elected in 1868.

Over in the Senate, Thad Stevens' resolution at first ran into trouble. Senator Doolittle of Wisconsin insisted, "All of these great questions concerning reconstruction, pacification, and the restoration of civil government in the Southern states, or anything which pertains to the federal relations of the United States with the several states, ought to be referred to the Judiciary Committee. Such has been the practice of this government from the beginning."

But Thad Stevens had his man in the Senate, one of the greatest minds in the country, and so different from Stevens in character that it is almost unbelievable that the two men could have had anything in common.

A child of Boston aristocracy, Charles Sumner had entered Boston Latin High School at the age of eleven, and Harvard at thirteen. He was writing for the *Boston Law Quarterly* while still a student in law school. After three years of legal research in Europe, he was elected to the U.S. Senate in 1848 by a coalition of anti-slavery Whigs, Free Soilers, and anti-slavery Democrats.

In the Senate, Sumner soon demonstrated his tenacity to principle. From the day he took his seat, the Massachusetts intellectual constantly spoke against slavery, the Fugitive Slave Law, and the Kansas-Nebraska Act. Sumner was not a flamboyant orator. His speeches were cool, restrained, and factual. But they hurt! They hurt so much that in 1852 Sumner was warned that his life was in danger.

Then, beginning on May 19, 1856, Sumner made a two-day speech on the Kansas problem in which he focussed his fire on Senator Butler of South Carolina. Two days later, while Sumner was alone in the Senate chamber working on some papers, Preston Brooks, a South Carolina representative, and a nephew of Senator Butler, entered the Chamber. After accusing Sumner of libelling his uncle, he beat Sumner over the head with a heavy cane until the Senator fell to the floor with a fractured skull. It was three years before Charles Sumner could return to the Senate, but Massachusetts refused to replace him.

In 1864, when President Lincoln had sent a bill to Congress recognizing the state government of Louisiana, Sumner had talked it to death in a one-man filibuster. Now Sumner adroitly piloted the Stevens resolution through the Senate, and after a heated debate, the resolution passed 33-11.

The Senate then turned its attention to the only territory it could govern directly, the District of Columbia. Here was the only place where the Republican majority could vote the franchise to the Negro. In the Southern states, it could only withhold representation in Congress if Negroes were not allowed to vote. The debate was long and fiery. Charges, claims, and arguments were made which were to be heard over and over again during the next eight years. The heroism of the Negro soldiers in the Union Army was reviewed. It was pointed out that Negroes were now taxpayers. The number of Negro churches and new Negro schools was cited. It was emphasized that Negroes had the right to vote in all but one of the original thirteen states under the Articles of Confederation. The final argument of the District Bill's backers was that voting Negroes in the nation's capital would be just punishment for hundreds of subversive traitors in the District who had aided the South at every turn during the War.

One speaker said, "Meaner rebels than many in this District could scarcely be found in the whole land. They have not been punished. The halter has been cheated of their necks. . . . But Congress in this District has the power to punish by ballot. . . . Sir, let it be applied. The rebels will recoil from it with horror. Some of the worst of them, rather than submit to black suffrage, will doubtless leave the District, and thus render an unspeakable service. . . ."

Another speaker replied, "You say to the Negroes, 'You have no right to vote in these states, but if you will go to Washington you can vote there.' I can see them swarming up from different sections of the country and inquiring where the polls are. Agents, men and women, such as there are at work in this city, will no doubt be at work in these states, telling them to pack their knapsacks and march to Washington, for on such a day there is to be an election, and there they will have the glorious privilege of the white man. . . ."

Meanwhile, the same lengthy debate on the District Bill had been going on in the House, and when the orators had become hoarse, a vote was taken. It passed, 116-54. But the Democrats in the Senate had talked with Andrew Johnson. The President had told them that he was hewing to Lincoln's policy: education first, then the vote. He would veto the bill. Word of Johnson's promise was passed around the Senate. Here the Radicals had less power than in the House. Charles Sumner had less influence than Thad Stevens. The Senate was not yet ready for an open break with the White House. Consequently, the District Bill was sent back to committee, and action was deferred until the second session of the Thirty-ninth Congress.

Now Congress was confronted with its first civil rights bill. The Thirteenth Amendment had made Lincoln's Emancipation Proclamation the law of the land. Slavery could never be practiced again. But the Amendment, containing only a few sentences, now needed to be spelled out by law.

The Civil Rights Bill, introduced by Senator Trumbull of Connecticut, was, on its face, even broader than that sponsored by Presidents Kennedy and Lyndon Johnson. It didn't even have a "Mrs. Murphy's boarding house" clause. But it was much less specific. There was no word on segregation. Although it seemed to cover every area of civil rights it failed to specify any particular applications. Considering the importance of such legislation, it is remarkable that the debate was much less lengthy than on the District Bill enabling Washington Negroes to vote. The roll call on the bill was: For, 33; Against, 12.

In the House, after lengthy debate over several amendments by moderates who feared a Presidential veto, the Civil Rights Bill was passed by a vote of 111 to 38. Twelve days later, on the twenty-seventh of March, the Clerk of the Senate read President Johnson's veto message.

The veto message was a carefully written document. There is evidence that Johnson wrote much better than he spoke. This was apparent when the transcripts of some of his impromptu speeches were produced at the trial. Johnson's objections to the Civil Rights Bill boiled down to the following reasons. First, that the Bill interfered with the rights of states to enact their own election laws involving state offices. Second, the Bill set aside from one class of people the naturalization laws of the United States. Johnson maintained that the Bill discriminated in favor of the recently freed Negro field hand, and against the well-educated European who must wait five years before applying for citizenship.

Johnson said, "The policy of the government . . . seems to have been that persons that are strangers to and unfamiliar with our institutions should pass through a certain probation, at the end of which, before attaining the coveted prize, they must give evidence of their fitness to receive and to exercise the rights of citizens. . . ."

After cries of "despot" in the Senate, and "dictator" in the House, the Civil Rights Bill was passed over Andrew

Johnson's veto by as heavy a majority as at its original passage.

The break between Congress and the White House was now wide open. It was clear that the President would veto every Reconstruction bill passed by the Republican majority. To the Republican leadership, this was pure treason. The Republicans had elected Johnson. Now he was following the Democratic line. Johnson contended that he was following the Lincoln line. Congress had demonstrated that it had the votes to override any Presidential veto, so if Johnson wanted war with Congress he could have it.

In the White House, the President was not an angry man. In his opinion, he was carrying out what Abraham Lincoln would have wanted. His conscience was clear. He was enjoying his meals, going to parties, sleeping well, and taking his daily rides in Rock Creek Park. He would continue to veto the bills he considered undesirable.

The next serious conflict between the President and Congress came over the voting rights of all those who had supported the Confederacy. Johnson had taken the position that Southerners who had taken part in the War could not vote until they had taken the "Amnesty Oath." This oath was a printed form prepared by the President. In substance, the applicant swore renewed allegiance to the United States, renounced the Confederacy, and promised never again to bear arms against the federal government. Upon completion of the oath, the President might grant a pardon restoring the applicant's full citizenship.

At the time Andrew Johnson was issuing Presidential

pardons wholesale. He believed it was Lincoln's way. He was convinced that it was the only way to restore responsible leadership to the South. How could the South recover when a man such as Wade Hampton, owning the greatest private library in the South, could not vote because he had been a Confederate general? The South needed the leadership of such good minds as college president Robert E. Lee, and former Confederate Vice President and constitutional authority Alexander Stephens. There could be no Reconstruction with the carpetbaggers in control.

On "The Hill" Congress raged. The President was exalting the men who had killed their sons and brothers at Gettysburg. Johnson was making possible the reactivation of the Confederacy. He was paving the way for Civil War II. He must be stopped.

Now Thad Stevens' Joint Committee on Reconstruction made its long awaited report. It accused Johnson of withholding vital information on the condition of the South. It reported Johnson's blunt statement that the states which had been in rebellion had never ceased to be states, and had been entitled to representation in Congress from the day they laid down their arms. Johnson had said that the Civil Rights Bill was unconstitutional because it had not been voted on by the states which it affected. The report concluded with the recommendation that, since former Confederate leaders were winning state elections over men who had remained loyal, no Southern states were ready for representation in Congrss.

The Reconstruction Committee's report came in the closing days of the session, and received noisy approval. Now, just before the adjournment of the Thirty-ninth

Congress, Thad Stevens struck his final blow of the session. He introduced what he called his Reconstruction Bill. The bill directed that, since the governments in the former Confederate states were illegal, they be disbanded; and that the South be divided into military districts, to be ruled and administered by the War Department.

It was the old story, a four-to-one affirmative vote in both houses, a Presidential veto, and an override. Thad Stevens was a very happy man, but there was one man even happier—Secretary of War Edwin M. Stanton.

8 · OUT-AGAIN-IN-AGAIN STANTON

It would require a psychiatrist rather than an author to describe Secretary of War Edwin M. Stanton accurately. A man of great ability, possessing an enormous capacity for hard work, he was a political trickster, a disloyal Cabinet member, and an emotionally unstable man. Stanton had entered Lincoln's Cabinet as Attorney General, and had served the President well. Then scandals in Simon Cameron's War Department rocked Washington. The Department was buying shoddy clothing for the Army at exhorbitant prices. Boots purchased from profiteering contractors fell apart as soon as they got wet. Lincoln had never trusted Cameron, but the crafty politician had delivered the Pennsylvania delegation to Lincoln at the 1860 Republican National Convention, and he had to be paid off. When the War profits scandals reached Lincoln's attention, he immediately asked Cameron to resign; and in his place he appointed Stanton.

From the day Stanton took the oath as Secretary of War, no breath of scandal ever touched that department which reflected on the Secretary's honesty and devotion to duty. The Army was magnificently equipped, and there was a huge stockpile of reserve supplies.

Edwin M. Stanton loved Lincoln—in a way. This is evidenced by his passion to serve his chief, and his emotional collapse immediately following the assassination. On the other side of the picture, and behind the President's back, he called the President "a baboon," criticized his conduct of the War, and his softness toward the South. By the end of Lincoln's first term, Stanton was fully in league with the Radicals.

Abraham Lincoln's temperament could endure a Stanton. Andrew Johnson could not. Lincoln knew what Stanton called him behind his back. He tolerated Stanton's interference in other departments, particularly the Navy. He passed over the known fact that Stanton was plotting with General McLellan against the President, and Lincoln knew that Stanton was using the recently-organized Secret Service to spy on other Cabinet mambers rather than on the Confederacy.

With all of this, Lincoln deeply appreciated Stanton's ability. There had never been a more dedicated, efficient, hard-working Secretary of War in the nation's history. With Stanton in the Secretaryship, the President never had to worry about the War Department. Stanton was there six days, and many times every day of the week, from soon after daybreak until late at night. He transacted his business standing behind an old-fashioned school master's desk. In a day before typewriters, dictaphones, duplicating machines and photostats, an enormous volume of paper work rolled out of the War Department. And Stanton expected all the staff in the Department to drive themselves as he did. When Abraham Lincoln completed his first term in the White House, it was natural that he should wish to retain his Secretary of War.

After Lincoln's assassination, Andrew Johnson, the new President, asked the entire Cabinet to remain in office. At first he was pleased with Stanton's cooperation, the supervision of the funeral arrangements, and the organization of the Grand Review after Appomattox. But then came the first unpleasant incident, Stanton's premature release of the Johnston surrender terms to the N.Y. *Times*. Lincoln might have scolded Stanton for this, but Andrew Johnson's boiling point was much lower than Lincoln's. Johnson was a trusting person, and now he found that his Secretary of War could not be trusted. Presiding over the Senate at the other end of the Avenue, Johnson had not heard of Stanton's meddling in both the Navy and State Departments, of his conspiring with Army officers, his favoritism in commissioning officers, or of his withholding important information from the President. Johnson could not know that the Sherman incident was typical of Edwin M. Stanton.

Then came the Reconstruction Act, dividing the conquered South into military districts, ruled by officers of the U.S. Army. These officers were, of course, responsible to the Secretary of War, making Stanton the virtual "King of the South." The Lincoln-Johnson Reconstruction was to be administered by men wearing shoulder straps and swords. Now the lights which burned bright in the War Department no longer illuminated a Secretary poring over contracts for rifles, drugs, coffins, and cannon. They now lit the nightly meetings between Stanton, Thad Stevens, Ben Butler, Charles Sumner, and the other Radical leaders in Congress. From his bedroom window in the White House, those lights were observed by Andrew Johnson, and he suspected that they were burning for no reason advantageous to his administration.

Next, Johnson's suspicion of Stanton increased because of the rapid change in his behavior at Cabinet meetings. During Lincoln's administration Stanton had been the most vocal member of the Cabinet. At its meetings, he dominated the discussions. He was brimming over with advice for the President, for all of the Cabinet departments, to the irritation of the Secretaries. He had acted similarly during the early months of Johnson's administration. Now he was becoming silent.

In the past, Cabinet officers had not confined to their own departments their advice to the President. Lincoln had written to Secretary of State Seward, "When a general line of policy is adopted, upon points arising in its progress, I wish, and suppose I am entitled to have, the advice of the Cabinet." When asked, Johnson's Cabinet had given counsel on national, and foreign affairs generally. Now, they continued to do so—all except Edwin M. Stanton. If asked by the President what he thought about a threatened revolution in Nicaragua, he only pulled his voluminous beard and shrugged his shoulders. In the rest of the Cabinet Johnson had complete confidence—but not in Stanton.

Now, the almost nightly meetings of the Radicals had shifted from the War Department to Thad Stevens' parlor where his mulatto housekeeper, Lydia Smith, served drinks. Ever since the opening of the Thirty-eighth Congress in December, 1865, the Radicals had determined that Andrew Johnson must go. His swiftness in reorganizing the Southern state governments and accepting their new constitutions convinced them that their plan for the South could never prevail with Johnson in the White House. But what could be done? There was no precedent. A President had never been removed. And even with Johnson's unpopularity throughout the North, the people would demand very potent reasons before insisting, before the world, that the United States must impeach a President whom they had elected.

The attempt at the opening of the December session had failed, and there were certainly not enough votes in the Senate to find Johnson guilty. No, the time was not ripe. There must be an incident, or a series of incidents, shocking enough to jolt the Northern public into supporting impeachment proceedings.

Charles Sumner suggested that Johnson's ineffective campaign against the Ku Klux Klan might be used as an issue. But Ben Butler disagreed, saying it might reflect against Stanton as Secretary of War rather than on "that man in the White House." Then Thad Stevens commented on the coolness between Stanton and the President. "Has it ever occurred to you, Edwin, that he might try to remove you?"

"I think that is highly probable," Stanton replied.

Butler licked his lips. "That would give us our chance."

But Charles Sumner counseled caution—they must be sure first. The support of the public for impeachment would depend on who Johnson might nominate to replace Stanton. He cautioned that the public would not support impeachment if Johnson should appoint, for instance, General of the Armies Ulysses S. Grant. That would only raise Johnson's sagging popularity.

Could it have been that Charles Sumner was a mind-reader, as well as an eminent statesman?

In the White House, Andrew Johnson had decided that Stanton must go. After the passage of the Reconstruction Act, he simply couldn't have as the man responsible for the military rule of the South one who was barely on speaking terms with him. Johnson also knew of Stanton's frequent secret meetings with the Radicals. No President could long retain in his Cabinet an official who was completely at odds with his policies. Conflicts of this nature had been dealt with in other administrations. A Cabinet officer was entitled to his honest opinion, and it might be the direct opposite of the President's. When this happened, the Cabinet officer resigned, with no bad feelings on either side. In case he did not, the President asked for his resignation, and it was submitted with no outward rancor. Andrew Johnson at that time believed that if he were asked, Stanton would step down.

Johnson was proud of his Cabinet, and wanted to retain its high standard of statesmanship. The man to replace Stanton must be of the highest caliber. Johnson knew that as a Democrat he could not be elected to a second term, so he had no political debts to pay. He was free to pick the best man in either party, but he preferred to choose a man who was not a political figure. The choice was easy— Ulysses S. Grant. No one could suggest a better, more qualified man to administer the War Department. Politically, Grant had failed to vote in any election before 1864. And Grant and Johnson were friendly at this point. Moreover, the choice would be popular with Congress, the people, and the Army.

Grant's first answer was "No." He knew nothing about the workings of government outside the Army. He had no patience with politicians, and wouldn't be able to get along with Congress. He didn't like being cooped up in an office. But Johnson argued that it should be a relief to get out of a uniform, and the rigid protocol of the Army. Grant hadn't seen much of his family in the past four years. Now he could buy a house in Washington and live a normal family life. As for the politicians, who would commit political suicide by opposing the greatest military hero since George Washington? Grant wanted to discuss the offer with his wife, but soon he wrote Johnson that he would accept the appointment providing his appointment could be accomplished without bitterness or political wrangling. Now it was only a question of the proper time for the change-over.

The scene now shifts to Capitol Hill. Andrew Johnson had not kept his intentions toward Secretary Stanton to himself. In fact, feeling the need of advice and support, he had "felt out" several members of his Cabinet. He had also talked with Chief Justice Chase about Stanton's removal. The Chief Justice agreed that the situation, with

Maj. Gen. U. S. Grant

Gen. W. T. Sherman

Stanton in the Cabinet, was impossible. He warned Johnson that he would be severely attacked by the Radicals
and the press, but thought Grant's appointment would have
almost nation-wide approval.

When anyone outside a President's own personal staff
is in on a secret, it is probable that there will be a "leak."
As centers for the exchange of White House gossip, the
Washington saloons of 1866 were no different from the
cocktail lounges of today. Swiftly the word got around that
the President would soon oust Stanton. The Radicals had
been waiting for the word, and this was it. Toward such
an eventuality, they had already drafted, and were ready
to present, a bill called The Tenure of Office Bill.

The bill, obviously unconstitutional, would prevent the
President from removing, while Congress was in session,
any official who had been appointed "with advice and
consent of the Senate." The bill was based on the reason-
ing that if a person, whether a Cabinet Secretary or village
postmaster, achieved his office only after approval by the
Senate, he could be removed only by the same process.
This obviously would tie the hands of any President whose
political party did not control the Senate. It violated every
principle of the President's responsibility for the executive
branch of the government. But no sooner had the rumors
of Edwin M. Stanton's removal reached the ears of Thad
Stevens than the Tenure Bill was promptly passed by both
the House and Senate. At the White House, the Tenure
Bill received a swift veto. Then Congress, just as swiftly,
passed it over the President's veto.

Now Andrew Johnson was ready for the final battle
which he had known was coming for a long time. He told

Horace Greeley, the influential editor of the New York *Tribune*, "If this means impeachment, I'm ready for the fight." In August, 1867, he called General Grant to the White House. He told him that he was ready to dismiss Stanton immediately and appoint Grant the new Secretary of War. Grant was reluctant. He had already said that he did not want to be embroiled in a political fight. Johnson pleaded that the quick action was necessary in order to throw the Tenure of Office Act into the Supreme Court where it most assuredly would be found unconstitutional.

Grant finally accepted the appointment. But when the order removing Stanton reached the War Department, the Secretary just laughed at it and locked himself in his office.

When the news of Grant's appointment reached the press, and Capitol Hill, it was apparent that Chief Justice Chase had underestimated the venom of the Radicals. Heretofore, Grant had been the idol of the nation, the darling of the Grand Army of the Republic, and criticism of this great military man was almost treasonable. But now he was being called a drunkard, a butcher at the Battle of the Wilderness, and the husband of a Southern wife. For a few days there were two Secretaries of War, and the generals in command of the Southern military districts could take their choice as to which they would obey. But the Ulysses Grant so fearless on the battlefield could not take the oppressive political situation. He "chickened out," and withdrew from the War Department.

Andrew Johnson was irate at this action of his old friend. He had believed that he could rely on "General U.S." who had always resented the petulant proddings of Stanton. Now Johnson was temporarily stymied. He had not talked with any other possible successor to Stanton but Grant. He had not licked the Tenure Act. There had to be a Secretary of War, so he reinstated Stanton. Naturally, relations between the President and the Secretary of War were more impossible than ever. Johnson had to decide quickly on another candidate to replace Stanton.

Johnson's second choice was as logical as his first. He selected the North's No. 2 hero, Lieutenant General William Tecumseh Sherman. How could anyone oppose Sherman's appointment while the song *Marching Through Georgia* was on the lips of every Yankee veteran? And so "Cump" Sherman was called to the White House. The President offered the same arguments which he had presented to Grant: a comfortable civilian life; good pay ($8,000 per year); and who among the Radicals would attack the man who had fought his way with 60,000 men, and no supply train, from Atlanta to the sea?

But "Cump" was adamant. He abhorred politics even more than Grant, and was later to say, when offered the Republican Presidential nomination, "I will not run, and will not serve if elected." Furthermore, Sherman had a divided loyalty. His brother, John, was sitting as U.S. Senator from Ohio, and was mildly aligned with the Radicals. Sherman didn't even ask for time to consider Johnson's offer. His answer was an emphatic "No!"

So Johnson was blocked again. Like the Radicals, who had been waiting for an issue, Johnson must have an incident which would prove to the nation that Stanton was unfit to be Secretary of War.

The incident didn't come, and Stanton was becoming more and more defiant of the President. Then Johnson had an idea. He had not forgotten the heckling over the New Orleans riot which he had received on his Mid-Western tour. Ever since the riot he had believed that there had been "something rotten in Denmark." The pieces of the puzzle just didn't fit together. He would never be satisfied until he really knew what happened on Canal Street. He meant to have the answer, and he instructed Colonel Moore, his personal secretary, to obtain from the War Department the entire correspondence file on the New Orleans incident.

The file was bulky, and for several nights Andrew Johnson, until he fell asleep, read on through every scrap of paper. Then one night he found the answer—General Baird's telegram to Secretary Stanton asking for instructions on the eve of the New Orleans riot. Where was Stanton's answer? It wasn't there! Now the picture was clear. Knowing that General Phil Sheridan was in Texas, Stanton had deliberately left Baird "out on a limb." A word from Stanton could have prevented the bloody riot. But Stanton had *wanted* that riot in order to discredit the President and add fuel to the fire of impeachment. Edwin Stanton had not acted on his own, Johnson was sure. He had been pressured by Ben Butler and Thad Stevens. The excuse for ousting Stanton from the War Department was not a damaging piece of paper which Johnson had been looking for. It was the absence of a piece of paper—instructions to General Baird. Two hundred Negro lives had been sacrificed because Thad Stevens wanted a riot which could be blamed on the President.

Andrew Johnson immediately called Stanton on the carpet. What excuse did he have for not issuing instructions to Baird, and why had he allowed Sheridan to go to Texas in the face of an impending race war? Stanton, though emotionally disturbed on occasion, seldom got angry, and he shrugged his shoulders in reply. He had confidence in Baird, he said, and he hadn't believed that Baird needed instructions. He would expect Baird to do the right thing at the right time.

Andrew Johnson proceeded to administer the most severe tongue-lashing ever received by a Cabinet officer. But the inscrutable Stanton remained unmoved, and he left the President's office smiling.

Johnson knew that he must act at once, for a Cabinet officer who would accept such a tirade from a President without immediately submitting his resignation would never willingly give up his office. Stanton must be ousted, and the Tenure of Office Act tested before the Supreme Court. But again, who should replace Stanton? Grant and Sherman had been eliminated. Johnson discovered that the Radicals had been to Grant, and told him that he might have the Republican nomination for President in 1868 if he remained clear of the Johnson-Stanton controversy. Grant, who heretofore had disliked politics, was suddenly bitten by the "Presidential bug." Among the military men, Sheridan was next in line, but he was openly allied with Stanton and the Radicals. There was also General George H. Thomas, but he was a Virginian, and would never be confirmed by the Senate.

Last on Johnson's list, but the most available, was Major General Lorenzo Thomas, Adjutant General of the Army. The aging Thomas was an efficient "paper work" general. He had only a meager record of combat command. Recently Stanton had sent him out on a trip to inspect and report on the condition of military cemeteries. A colorless figure, Thomas nevertheless knew the routine workings of the War Department. Today, a critic of our Defense Department would refer to a Thomas as "Pentagon brass." But Thomas had no enemies, and Johnson sent for him.

No, Thomas said, he would prefer not to take over as Secretary of War. He and Stanton had always been friendly. Moreover, he was perfectly happy as Adjutant General, and would like to stay in his office until retirement. By now, Andrew Johnson was impatient with generals who in the past had taken orders, but now felt privileged to do as they pleased. Wasn't he their Commander-in-Chief? Johnson brought the interview to an abrupt close, and told Thomas that he was to return the following day—February 21, 1868.

Thomas returned to his office in the War Department and went straight to Secretary Stanton's office, where he asked if he might issue the customary order closing the department offices on Washington's Birthday. Stanton approved the order, and then asked if Thomas had been to the White House. Thomas lied, saying he had been there to deliver papers from General Grant.

The next day, February 21, while Secretary Stanton was closeted with Stevens, Butler, and Sumner, General Alonzo Thomas returned to the White House, and was ushered into the President's office by Colonel Moore. Johnson came to the point immediately: "General Thomas," he said, "Colonel Moore, at my command, has prepared two orders for you. One is to be delivered to Secretary Stanton at once. Colonel Moore, you will read the orders to General Thomas."

Colonel Moore read:

"Executive Mansion, Washington, D.C.
"To the Honorable Edwin M. Stanton, Washington, D.C.
"Sir: By virtue of the power and authority vested in me as President by the Constitution and laws of the United States, you are hereby removed from office as Secretary of War, and your functions will terminate on the receipt of this communication. You will transfer to Major General Lorenzo Thomas, who has this day been authorized and empowered to act as Secretary of War *ad interim*, all records, books, papers, and other property now in your custody and charge.
"Respectfully yours,
ANDREW JOHNSON"

Colonel Moore then read the second order:

"To Major General Lorenzo Thomas,
"Adjutant General, U.S. Army, Washington, D.C.
"Sir: Edwin M. Stanton having this day been removed from the office of Secretary of War, you are hereby authorized and empowered to act as Secretary of War *ad interim*, and will immediately enter upon the discharge of the duties pertaining to that office.
"Respectfully yours,
ANDREW JOHNSON"

This time, Thomas realized that the President was in no mood to discuss whether or not the appointment was agreeable to him. Johnson was acting as Commander-in-Chief. Thomas saluted and said, "Sir, I will do my best to support the Constitution and the nation's laws."

Then the President took from his desk another paper and handed it to Thomas. "This, General, you will deliver to the Senate after you have taken over Stanton's office." Thomas read the paper, a letter to the President *pro tempore* of the Senate notifying the Senate of Johnson's orders to Stanton and Thomas. Then Thomas spoke, "But, Mr. President, won't the Senate invoke the Tenure of Office Act?"

"That's just what I want," Johnson snapped.

9 · THE EXPLOSION

The fuse had been lit on February 20. The explosion came on the twenty-first. On that day General Thomas left the White House and went straight to his office in the War Department. He didn't relish the task ahead of him. He was one of the few people who really liked Edwin M. Stanton, and Stanton liked him. In the past, when fatigue or emotional stress made it necessary for the Secretary to take a "breather," he would call Thomas to his office. The pair would exchange jokes. Stanton would take a bottle from his desk drawer and pour drinks. Sometimes he would even rumple Thomas's hair. Now Thomas had the unpleasant task of turning his friend out of the office he had held for five years. Also Thomas did not look forward to being a guinea pig in a test of the Tenure Act.

Anticipating the day when he would be questioned on the manner of Stanton's removal, Thomas took with him as a witness General Williams, one of the assistant adjutants general. In Stanton's office, Thomas was greeted cordially. With no preliminary explanation, Thomas handed the President's order to Stanton. The Secretary adjusted his small, steel-rimmed spectacles, and read.

Without comment, or change of facial expression, Stanton said, "Do you wish me to vacate the office at once, or will you give me time to remove my private property?"

Thomas later testified at the trial that he replied, "At your pleasure."

At that moment General Grant entered the Secretary's office. He sensed that something momentous was happening, and he looked inquiringly from Thomas to Stanton. Colonel Thomas answered the look by handing Grant the order. Grant asked if the order was for him. Thomas said no, it was just for his information, but he would have a copy made for Grant's records. The General of the Armies shifted his cigar to the other side of his mouth and said, "I do not know whether I will obey your instructions or whether I will resist them."

After having the copy of the order made for Grant in the Adjutant's office, Thomas returned to Stanton's office an hour later. Stanton was there, but not at his desk. Thomas sat down at the desk and, in an even tone, told the former (?) Secretary that he would proceed to issue orders from the War Department. Stanton calmly told him that he would not, and that he, Stanton, would countermand any orders Thomas issued. Then Stanton handed Thomas a paper which read:

War Department
Feb. 21, 1868
Major General Lorenzo Thomas, Adjutant General
Sir: I am informed that you presume to issue orders
as Secretary of War *ad interim*. Such conduct and
orders are illegal, and you are hereby commanded to
abstain from issuing any orders other than in your
capacity as Adjutant General of the Army.

Your obedient servant,
EDWIN M. STANTON
Secretary of War

Thomas stuffed the paper from his disobedient friend in
his pocket, and left for the White House. There he asked
to see the President. Reading the order from Stanton,
Johnson smiled and said that he had expected it. Thomas
asked for instructions. There was testimony at the trial
that Johnson said, "If he doesn't get out, we'll kick him
out," but the statement was never proven. Thomas claimed
that the President only told him to stand by for further
instructions.

By this time, the Senate had adjourned for the day, and
Thomas could not deliver the President's announcement to
Ben Wade, President *pro tempore*. Thomas spent the rest
of the day in the Adjutant's office, and went to bed early
that night. At eight the next morning, before the General
had eaten his breakfast, there were loud knocks at his front
door. Opening it, he was faced by the U.S. Marshal for
the District of Columbia, two assistant marshals, and a con-
stable. The U.S. Marshal said, "General Thomas, you are
under arrest. Come with me."

General Thomas asked that he be taken to the White House before appearing in court. He only wanted the President to know that he had been arrested. The Marshal agreed, provided that Thomas never be out of his sight. Andrew Johnson again was not surprised, he was even pleased. "This is just where we want it," he said, "in the courts." He said that he would provide Thomas with lawyers, and that bail, if any, would be paid. Up to this time, General Thomas was wholly ignorant of the charges against him.

From the White House, the Marshal took the General to the District Municipal Court. There he was arraigned before Judge Carter on a complaint, signed by Secretary of War Stanton, accusing him of "wilfully and maliciously trying to take possession of the Secretary of War's office." Thomas pleaded not guilty, and Judge Carter set his bail at $5,000. The bail was provided by the prominent New York attorney, William M. Evarts, the man President Johnson had assigned to represent Thomas. Evarts would also represent the President at the impeachment trial.

Next came a scene which properly belonged in a comic opera rather than in a knock-down-drag-out struggle of power politics. Released from the custody of the court, Thomas headed straight for the War Department, and Secretary Stanton's office. He found Stanton engaged in a heated conversation with a group of Radicals from the House. Upon Thomas's appearance, the congressmen withdrew. Stanton, as always, greeted Thomas warmly, and asked the object of his visit. Thomas replied, "The next time you have me arrested, please do not do it before I get something to eat."

Then the unpredictable Stanton rose, put an arm around Thomas's shoulder, and rumpled his hair. He called out to his military aide in the next office, "General Schriver, uncork that bottle of brandy I just bought for the Adjutant General, and bring three glasses." How long this trio stayed with the bottle of brandy was never brought out at the trial, but again General Thomas was too late to deliver Andrew Johnson's announcement of the removal of Stanton to the Senate. It was Washington's Birthday, and the Senate, after listening to the traditional reading of Washington's Farewell Address, had adjourned for the day.

While the Senate was considering routine legislation on February 21, and preparing to celebrate Washington's Birthday, the House was getting things done. General Thomas had no more than left Stanton's office to have a copy of Johnson's order made for Grant, when a messenger left the War Department with a note for Thad Stevens. Within less than an hour, the long-awaited news had been passed to every Radical in the House: "It has happened at last—what we have been waiting for these three long years."

That afternoon, Thad Stevens dragged his club foot to the center aisle of the House and announced, "Upon the evidence collected by the Committee on Reconstruction, which is herewith presented, and in virtue of the powers with which they have been invested by the House, they are of the opinion that Andrew Johnson, President of the United States, be impeached of high crimes and misdemeanors. They therefore recommend to the House the adoption of the following resolution: RESOLVED, that

The Andrew Johnson Impeachment Committee. The principal mover of this group, Thaddeus Stevens (second from left, seated) was mortally sick when this picture was taken. Standing left to right: J. F. Wilson, G. S. Boutwell, J. A. Logan. Seated: Ben Butler, Stevens, Wm. J. Bingham.

Andrew Johnson, President of the United States, be impeached of high crimes and misdemeanors in office."

February 22 being a Saturday, and the Senate not having received President Johnson's announcement of Stanton's dismissal on that day, the impeachment vote in the House did not come until Monday the twenty-fourth. Everyone knew the outcome. The Tenure of Office Act had been violated by the President. Johnson had openly insulted Congress, they said. He had wilfully broken a law. The vote on Monday was overwhelmingly for impeachment: Yeas, 126; Nays, 47; Not voting, 17. Even House Speaker Colfax stepped down from the chair, enabling himself to vote with the majority.

The first and only impeachment of a President of the United States had been voted.

10 · THE RULES OF THE GAME

As soon as unofficial word reached the Senate that the impeachment resolution had passed the House, there was but one topic of conversation between the senators gathered in the hotel lobbies, congressional boarding-houses, and saloons of Washington. It was: "How do we go about it?" There had been only three impeachments tried by the Senate in the history of the nation. These three all involved federal district judges, and were fairly simple. One judge was found guilty of drunkenness on the bench; the second, illegal imprisonment of defense counsel during a trial; and the third for using improper language on the bench. In the three cases, the evidence for conviction had been overwhelming.

But how to try a President? The authors of the Consti-

tution had been mum on the subject of how to conduct
an impeachment trial, except for specifying that, when a
President is tried, the Chief Justice of the Supreme Court
must preside over the Senate. Congress had never enacted
a law setting up an impeachment trial procedure. The
senators asked each other, "Shall the rules of the Senate
prevail, or the rules of a court of law? Are we a jury,
fifty-four judges, or are we still senators? What happens
to Ben Wade as President *pro tempore* of the Senate?
Whose responsibility is it to draw up a trial procedure?
And what does Salmon Chase have to say about it?"

The senators were still asking these questions when on
February 25, at noon, the gaunt, aged, sick Thaddeus
Stevens appeared at the bar of the Senate and read, "Mr.
President, in obedience to the order of the House of Representatives, we appear before you, and in the name of
the House of Representatives and of all the people of the
United States we do impeach Andrew Johnson, President
of the United States, of high crimes and misdemeanors; and
we further inform the Senate that the House will in due
time exhibit particular articles of impeachment against him
and make good the same. . . ."

The full articles of impeachment did not reach the Senate
until Wednesday, March 4. There were eleven articles
(charges) in all, and they occupied five pages of fine print.
Most of the articles were repetitious, simply rephrasings
of the basic charges. The 1500 words in the document,
boiled down, charged the President with violating the Tenure of Office Act; defaming the good name of Congress
in his speeches at Cleveland and St. Louis; appointing General Thomas Secretary of War without approval of the

Senate while it was in session; and issuing orders to Army officers without passing them through the Secretary of War.

The question of who would draft the rules for conducting the trial was quickly disposed of the next day, at one P.M. when Chief Justice Salmon P. Chase called the Senate to order. He brought the rules with him.

The Chief Justice's first act was to swear in each senator individually, using the oath: "I do solemnly swear that in all things appertaining to the trial of the impeachment of Andrew Johnson, President of the United States, I will do impartial justice to the Constitution and the laws—so help me God."

The first skirmish in the organization of the trial came when President *pro tempore* Ben Wade rose to take the oath. Before he could raise his right hand, Democratic Minority Leader Hendricks leaped to his feet and protested that, since Wade would succeed to the Presidency if Andrew Johnson were convicted, it was highly improper for Wade to vote on conviction. This threw the Senate into a partisan uproar, and the body adjourned for the day.

That night Ben Wade was the subject of debate in the Washington bars, dining rooms, and gambling houses. "Hendricks was right. Would anyone expect Ben Wade to vote himself out of the White House? This thing may be decided by one vote." But others said, "You can't prevent Wade from voting. Every state is entitled to representation by two senators. It wouldn't be constitutional for Ohio to have only one." The next day Hendricks, realizing that his objection was bound to be defeated on a strict partisan vote, withdrew his motion.

The same day, the Radicals in the Senate received their

first shock and setback. From the earliest talk of impeachment, they had been convinced that they had a friend in
Salmon P. Chase. He had, in all of his words and actions
outside the Supreme Court, backed Radical policies. As
Governor of Ohio, he had made the state a haven for
escaped slaves, to the extent that he earned the title "Attor-
ney-General for Runaway Negroes." As Secretary of the
Treasury, he had opposed Lincoln's policies, and he had
been the Radicals' choice to replace Lincoln as the Republican Presidential nominee in 1864. With Chase on the
bench in the Johnson trial, the Radicals would run things
their own way. Or so they thought. The Senate would
work under Senate rules, rules which could be changed at
any time during the trial by a roll call vote. But while the
Radicals thought they knew Chase, the man, they hadn't
reckoned with Chase, the lawyer.

Chase opened the proceedings of the day by informing
the senators that they were no longer sitting in the Senate,
they were in a court of law as jurors. However, since this
was no ordinary court, certain deviations from normal trial
procedure would be in order. The senators might ask questions of the witnesses provided they submitted their questions in writing. On challenged evidence, the senators, by
a roll call vote, might rule on whether it could be admitted.
The Senate would convene as a court each day except
Sunday at one P.M.

Now there was no question who was boss. The Radicals
grumbled, but some said, "It could have been worse. While
we can vote on what evidence can be admitted, we can
make it mighty hard for the defense."

❁❁

11 · TRIAL OR FARCE?

The scene is awesome, one never seen before or since. The Senate galleries are packed. All of Washington society is there. Admission is by ticket only, each senator being limited to four tickets per day throughout the trial. Some senators are selling tickets for as much as ten dollars per day. High on the Senate President's dais sits Chief Justice of the Supreme Court Salmon P. Chase, in his rich silk robe—a huge man, with a massive bald head, bushy eyebrows, and thick lips, a picture of the law's majesty.

Chase, a graduate of Dartmouth College, had early achieved an outstanding legal reputation, and had served as Governor of Ohio. An ardent Abolitionist, he had been one of the original Lincoln men at the 1860 Republican National Convention. For his support, and for carrying

Ohio, Lincoln had made him Secretary of the Treasury. With growing Presidential ambitions for 1864, Chase had been wooing the support of the Radicals. Lincoln had been at the point of dropping Chase from the Cabinet when Chief Justice Taney suddenly died. Immediately, Lincoln solved his Chase problem by "kicking him upstairs" to replace Taney.

Chase had made a fine record as Chief Justice. And he had another record, that of being the father of the most beautiful woman in Washington, Kate Chase Sprague, wife of Senator Sprague of Rhode Island.

Seated at two long tables in front of Justice Chase are the managers (counsel) for the prosecution, and the defense. All six managers for the prosecution are members of the House. Their chairman, Thad Stevens, is now near death. His eyelids droop, and his face is almost a death mask. His head, now merely a skull, is capped by an ill-fitting black wig. He is carried to his chair, and has turned over the direction of the prosecution to Ben Butler.

Searching the pages of history, including his own memoirs, it is impossible to find anyone who liked Benjamin Franklin Butler, unless it was his mother. He had been known during the Civil War as "Old Cock-eye," "Silver Spoons Ben," "Beast Butler," and "Bottled-up Butler."

"Silver Spoons" was earned during Butler's occupation of New Orleans in 1862. It was his custom to let it be known that the commanding general was available for dinner invitations. After consuming a dinner which his hosts could ill afford, the General confiscated the family silver on the grounds that the family had doubtless supported the

Confederacy in some way. Then Butler sold the silver in Massachusetts, and kept the money.

"Old Cock-eye," of course, referred to Butler's appearance. He was a short man, with a little paunch. He grew a villainous drooping mustache. One squinting eye peered straight ahead, while its twin enabled lawyer Butler to look both the judge and the jury in the eye at the same time.

"Beast" was also earned in New Orleans where the orders he issued were as ugly as Butler was himself.

"Bottled-up" came from Butler's inept strategy on the James River when he allowed Lee to prevent his army from coming to Grant's aid before Petersburg. Ben Butler had the legal razzle-dazzle of a Perry Mason, and a tongue dipped in nitric acid.

The other managers for the prosecution are George S. Boutwell of Massachusetts, John A. Logan of Illinois, a former War Democrat, and a former "political" major general; James F. Wilson of Iowa, John A. Bingham of Ohio, and Thomas Wilson of Pennsylvania.

On the other side of the Senate Chamber sit the managers for the defense. They are headed by Henry Stanberry. A former Associate Justice of the Supreme Court, Stanberry has just resigned as Johnson's Attorney General, in order that it may not be said that tax funds are being used to defend the impeached President. The other defense managers are Benjamin R. Curtis, Jeremiah S. Black (later to resign), William M. Evarts, and Thomas A. R. Nelson.

It is one P.M. on Friday, March 13 (unlucky for whom?) when Chief Justice Chase enters the Senate Chamber. The Sergeant-at-arms intones, "Hear ye! Hear ye! all persons

are comanded to keep silence while the Senate is sitting for
the trial of the articles of impeachment by the House of
Representatives against Andrew Johnson, President of the
United States."

The Sergeant-at-arms then introduces the managers to
the Senate. Next he offers proof that he has served a sum-
mons on Andrew Johnson to appear before the Senate.
He then reads the reply from Johnson authorizing his managers to act for him, and asking for at least forty days to
prepare his defense.

The President's request triggers an argument which con-
sumes the first day of the trial, and which is indicative of
the treatment which Andrew Johnson can expect from the
Senate. Ben Butler says that he is ready to open for the
prosecution this very minute. Attorney Stanberry argues
that the prosecution has been gathering evidence and witnesses for months, while the managers for the defense could
not be appointed until after the impeachment. He accuses
Butler of wanting the trial of the President conducted as
though it were "in a comon municipal court." He charges
the prosecution with trying to "railroad" the President. In
a characteristic Butler retort, the prosecution manager says,
"Well, this is the age of the railroads, isn't it?"

In reply to Andrew Johnson's request for forty days to
prepare a defense, a strict party-line vote gives him ten.
The defense is stunned.

The reopening of the trial on March 23 witnessed one
of the several futile attempts of the Democratic minority
to harass the prosecution. As soon as the Chief Justice called
the Senate to order, Senator Davis of Kentucky rose and
argued that, since not all of the states in the Union were

The Impeachment of Andrew Johnson

represented in the Senate, the impeachment trial could not be held, and he moved that the trial be adjourned. Davis's motion failed to get even all of the Democratic votes.

What kind of a trial was this in terms of the justice an ordinary citizen can expect in a court of law? Here was a jury of fifty-four men, three-quarters of whom any defense attorney would challenge. Here were at least thirty-three men who had been attacking the President on every Senate roll call for two years. What jury has ever been allowed to question witnesses, without any cross-examination by the defense? What jury has ever been empowered to rule on what evidence is admissible? Even though Chief Justice Chase had outlined a trial procedure, a roll call vote of the Senate could change it at any time—at any time when the defense seemed to be making headway.

The first order of business on March 23 was the reading of Andrew Johnson's reply to the impeachment charges. Actually prepared by Stanberry and signed by the President, the document revealed the former Attorney General's legal acumen. In his answer to the charge that Johnson had violated the Tenure of Office Act, Stanberry threw a legal bombshell from which the prosecution never fully recovered, although they tried to ignore it. Unwittingly, the Radicals had set a trap when they wrote the Act.

The Tenure of Office Act stated that, while Congress was in session, any office holder, appointed with the advice and consent of the Senate, could not be removed by the President without the same advice and consent. But the Radicals had added this paragraph: "*Provided*, that the Secretaries of State, of the Treasury, of War, of the Navy, and of the Interior, the Postmaster General and the Attorney General, shall hold their offices respectively for and during the term of the President by whom they have been appointed."

The Radicals had written this in haste, considering that Andrew Johnson was only serving out Lincoln's second term which did not expire until March 4, 1869. But now Stanberry called the Senate's attention to the fact that Lincoln had never bothered to *reappoint* Stanton at the beginning of his second term in 1865. Stanton was nothing but a holdover. Lincoln could have appointed a new Secretary of War at any time. Stanton had no claim whatsoever to his office. Furthermore Stanberry argued that, while Lincoln's term would have expired in March, 1869, had he lived, *death had ended that term* on April 15, 1865, and the Tenure of Office Act specifically gave Andrew Johnson the authority to appoint an entirely new Cabinet.

Attorney Stanberry now turned to the charge that the President had libeled Congress. He challenged the managers for the prosecution to produce verified copies of the Johnson speeches in Cleveland, St. Louis, and before the Union Party delegates. He charged that the only evidence the prosecution had was newspaper hearsay, unusable in court.

Having presented the President's answers to the impeachment articles, a document which covers twenty-four pages of fine print, Stanberry asked for thirty more days to assemble evidence and summon witnesses. He said that it had taken the ten days allowed him just to prepare the President's reply. John A. Logan, a manager for the prosecution, demanded that the trial begin immediately, charging that all Stanberry wanted was time to prepare endless speeches which would delay the proceedings. A motion was made to allow the defense thirty days for preparation. On a roll call vote, the motion was defeated 41-12.

It was the will of the Senate that Andrew Johnson go on trial immediately, without one day's preparation for defense. That night some of the senators remembered that they had consciences, and the following day the Senate voted to give the defense six more days until March 30, to prepare its case.

On March 30, Ben Butler opened for the prosecution, and spoke for three hours. It was thought that the snarling, pompous, little Massachusetts lawyer would be at his best. But witnesses later said that the speech was incredibly dull. Because of its length, Butler had to read the address, which robbed him of his usual fire. Before the end of the speech, many of the senators, lolling in their comfortable armchairs, were asleep, as was Thad Stevens, looking like a corpse.

Butler's speech was overloaded with the citing of impeachment trials going back to King John of England. But after this slow start Ben Butler turned from dull British legal history to the sarcasm of which he was a master. In lauding Stanton for refusing to leave his office, he said, "To desert it now would be to imitate his *accidental Chief*."

Turning to the charge that Johnson had libeled Congress on at least three different occasions, Butler declared that every would-be despot in history had first slandered his legislative bodies and weakened them in the eyes of the people before assuming dictatorship. Butler derided Johnson for his angry speech in Cleveland and quoted the alleged cries from the crowd: "Don't git mad, Andy," "Mind your dignity, Andy," and "Bully for you, Andy."

When the yawning senators had recovered from Butler's

three-hour tirade, the prosecution began presenting its evidence. The first day was occupied by filing as exhibits documents which everyone had read months before. The next day, the first witnesses were called, and it was immediately apparent that it would be a long trial.

In a normal courtroom trial, if the attorney for one side desires to keep out of evidence a question put to a witness by the opposing attorney, he rises and says to the judge, "I object, your honor." The judge then asks the examining attorney what he expects to prove by the question, and then rules whether the question just asked is objectionable or not. But under the rules of Andrew Johnson's trial, every objection had to be decided by a roll-call vote of the Senate. Furthermore, there was no limit on the time the opposing managers could spend debating the objections. From the opening of the trial on March 30 until its adjournment in May, far more time was consumed in taking roll calls on the admissibility of evidence than in questioning and cross-examining witnesses.

The testimony of the first witnesses was as boring as the reading of the long documents entered as exhibits. These witnesses were only government clerks who testified to what everyone already knew and the defense did not deny.

But the Senate got its occasional laughs along with its boredom. Ben Butler produced a "character" named George W. Karsner. Karsner's mission in life seems to have been publicizing the glories of his home state which was, as he put it, "The Great State of Delaware." At the time Andrew Johnson had appointed Lorenzo Thomas Secretary of War *ad interim,* Karsner came to Washington to see about getting a mail delivery contract in his home town of New

Castle. Since General Thomas was a native of Delaware, Karsner called on him. Karsner thought that all Delawareans should know each other—and in 1868, they probably should have.

The New Castle booster testified on the stand that General Thomas invited him to come along to a White House reception and meet the President. While they were waiting to be received by the President and his Cabinet, Karsner said that he and Thomas were discussing what the latter would do about Stanton if he refused to leave the War Department. He testified that Thomas had said he would call upon General Grant to send a detachment of troops to remove Stanton.

Defense manager Stanberry, in his cross-examination, asked Karsner what he said to Thomas at this point. Karsner's answer was: "I said, 'General, never forget—*The eyes of Delaware are upon you.*'"

Butler now disclosed by his questioning that his strategy would be to smear, before they were called to testify, the character of persons he knew would be star defense witnesses. Obviously Adjutant General Thomas would be one of these. It was noticeable during the testimony of Walter Burleigh, a delegate to Congress from the Dakota Territory, that this was Butler's scheme. Butler was trying to make Burleigh say that Andrew Johnson had conspired with Thomas to oust Stanton. Defense manager Evarts objected on the grounds that the President, not Thomas, was on trial.

On being asked by Chief Justice Chase what Butler was trying to prove, "Old Cock-eye" replied, "That was the first performance of the President, the first act in the drama.

He had to take a disgraced officer, and take away his disgrace, and put him into the Adjutant General's office, from which he had been removed by President Lincoln and Mr. Stanton, in order to get a fit instrument on which to operate. That was part of the training for the next stage. Having gotten him in that condition, he being sufficiently virulent toward Mr. Stanton for having suspended him from the office of Adjutant General, the President is then ready to appoint him Secretary *ad interim*, which he does within two or three days thereafter."

Having harped on Andrew Johnson's violation of the Tenure of Office Act for several days, manager Butler now turned to the charge that Johnson had conspired to take the War Department by force, and had boasted that he could become a dictator if he wanted to. Butler further charged that Johnson had issued orders to Army officers without sending these orders through General Grant.

The first charge was ridiculous, but stemmed from the inaccurately reported and not-so-funny jibe Johnson had made in St. Louis: that if he really wanted to be a dictator, all he had to do was call on the Army. On the charge of issuing direct orders to officers, Johnson was vulnerable, but not criminal.

First, Butler called to the witness stand Colonel William H. Emory, a brevet major general, who was in command of the District of Washington. Emory testified that in September, 1867, the President had called him to the White House.

Question: "State as well as you can the substance of the conversation with the President."

Answer: "I can only give the substance of it. He asked

me about the strength of the troops, and I told him the location of each post, and, as near as I can recollect, the commanding officer of the post."

Colonel Emory further testified that the President wanted to know if it were not desirable to have more troops in Washington, and Emory had replied that the city should never be without a brigade of infantry, a battery of artillery, and a squadron of cavalry.

Asked if he had been called to the White House a second time, Emory testified that he had been there on February 22, 1868, the day after Stanton was removed. The President had asked Emory if he had followed the recommendations which he had made the previous September. Emory told Johnson that there were less troops in the capital than there had been in September. Several detachments had been sent elsewhere. Johnson asked Emory why he had not brought his troops up to full strength, and Emory replied that he had no orders to do so. Then, according to Emory, the President became angry, and asked if Emory didn't consider the conversation of the previous September as an order. Emory testified that he had told Johnson he could not accept orders from anyone other than General Grant. Then Emory said that Johnson had become furious, and asked Emory if he didn't recognize him as Commander-in-Chief.

Colonel Emory's testimony was undoubtedly damaging to Andrew Johnson. The picture of an angry President "throwing his weight around" as Commander-in-Chief in peace time is not a pretty one. Nevertheless, Johnson's position was difficult. Had he sent the order through Grant, the latter would have said that any order to him must come from the Secretary of War. Stanton had been removed the day before Johnson saw Emory, and Grant had intimated the previous day that he might refuse to recognize Lorenzo Thomas as Secretary of War. Johnson no longer felt that he could trust Grant.

Next, Butler called for the prosecution a string of witnesses who are interesting today, not for the importance of their testimony, but because they demonstrate the news coverage of Presidential speeches in 1866.

Today, when a President makes a major speech, the speech is written well in advance. It is mimeographed and handed to the wire services, TV, and radio before it is delivered. On-the-scene coverage of the speech is only to note deviations from the script which the President might make, audience reaction, and local color. But in 1866, there were no mimeographed handouts and no teletype machines. Except for messages to Congress, Andrew Johnson preferred to speak "off the cuff" rather than write speeches in advance.

First, Butler called a Western Union telegraph operator who handled dispatches for the Associated Press out of Washington. Today, a teletype machine would speed a Presidential address to every AP bureau in the country, but Butler's witness took a handwritten copy of a Johnson speech from an AP Capital correspondent, and tapped it out on his telegraph key. His message went to Baltimore from where it was relayed to other telegraph stations. The Washington telegrapher's testimony was confined to the transmission of Johnson's speech to the Union Party delegates.

Next, Butler called up the newspaper correspondents

who had reported Johnson's speeches in Cleveland, and St. Louis, where the President had allegedly slandered Congress. Here again we have a picture of 1866 news coverage and its accuracy. The latter provided a field day for the defense.

In those days of spread-eagle oratory, the shortest speech was long by present standards. It took a good extemporaneous speaker at least thirty minutes just to get warmed up. Thus, a verbatim report of a speech presented many problems to the news correspondent. Most of the reporters on the witness stand said that they used one of the several shorthand methods taught in the commercial colleges of the day. Some had devised their own methods. They testified that in long speeches it was common for the reporters from the newspapers present to work in relays. One reporter would take down thirty minutes of a speech, and then another would take over. After the speech, the reporters got together and pooled their notes. Manager Butler had newspaper copies of Johnson's Cleveland and St. Louis speeches entered as evidence.

Then defense manager Stanberry took over. On cross-examination of the newsmen, Stanberry produced transcripts of Johnson's speeches as reported in the St. Louis, Cleveland, New York, and Chicago newspapers, and *they varied greatly*. The correspondents admitted that audience reaction to Johnson's speeches was reported according to the politics of the newspapers for which they worked— "brought great applause" (Democratic), or "these words were received with cold silence" (Republican).

Stanberry asked the correspondents if, in the final telegraph draft, they had ever changed any of Andrew Johnson's words. Then the Senate got one of its rare laughs during the trial when the reporters admitted that they had made corrections in Johnson's grammar. It seemed that when Andrew Johnson became angry under heckling, he lapsed into those common grammatical errors which bring premature gray hairs to freshman high school English teachers. His most common error was using "don't" instead of "doesn't."

Stanberry probed further: since the newsmen had taken the liberty of correcting the President's grammar, had they possibly, at times, changed his sentence construction? The answer was "Yes." Then Stanberry asked, if they had changed Johnson's sentence construction, was it not possible that they had changed the meaning of sentences. The reporters did not think they had done so, but admitted that it was possible. Then the defense dismissed the newsmen with the conclusion that such a thing as an exact verbatim transcript of a Johnson speech had never been published.

The prosecution managers droned on until April 9, and closed their case. As the defense took over, manager Curtis reiterated what Judge Stanberry had said at the opening of the trial: that since Edwin M. Stanton had not been reappointed by President Lincoln at the opening of his second term, and was only a holdover from Lincoln's first term, Andrew Johnson had not violated the Tenure Act.

Then Curtis introduced very important evidence. After the House had passed the Tenure Act, the Senate had amended it. Thus it had to go back to a Senate-House conference committee for agreement. Curtis produced the minutes of those meetings, and they revealed that while the House members made no bones about the fact that their sole purpose was to keep Stanton in office, the senators violently disagreed. Curtis read a statement made by Senator Sherman of Ohio, purportedly a Radical, in which he said, "I say that the Senate have not legislated with a view to any persons, or any President, and therefore he [Representative Schenck] commences by stating what is not true. We do not legislate to keep in the Secretary of War, the Secretary of the Navy, or the Secretary of State."

As was expected, the first witness for the defense was Adjutant General Lorenzo Thomas. The man who had been Secretary of War for twenty-four hours proved to be a dull witness. However, his dullness enabled him to withstand the blistering cross-examination of Ben Butler. The snarling manager for the prosecution unsuccessfully pulled out every trick in his legal bag to confuse Thomas into contradicting himself.

Then he tried to make Thomas look ridiculous. At one point, Butler made Thomas admit that he had been "bragging or joking" when he told his Delaware friend, Karsner, that he might use force to remove Stanton from his office. From then on, after every statement by Thomas, Butler would ask, "I suppose you were bragging or joking again, General?"

The next morning ushered in a dark day for the prosecution as the defense asked the Sergeant-at-arms to bring in the next witness. There appeared in the doorway a short, wiry man, with a grizzled beard, gimlet eyes, and a tight mouth—Lieutenant General William Tecumseh Sherman.

Ben Butler immediately huddled with his fellow managers. Their strategy must be changed. They hadn't expected Sherman. They couldn't handle Sherman as they had handled Thomas. "Cump" Sherman could be most damaging. He hated Stanton, although refusing to serve in his place. No cross-examination could confuse the clear-thinking mind of the General. But worse yet, there was John Sherman, the General's brother, sitting there behind his desk as Senator from Ohio.

General Sherman had been on the stand but a few minutes when the new strategy of the prosecution became clear. Stanberry asked, "During that time, from December fourth until the third of February, had you several interviews with the President?"

Answer: "Yes, sir."

Question: "Had you several interviews with him in relation to the case of Mr. Stanton?"

Answer: "I had."

Prosecution manager Bingham leaped to his feet: "Mr. Chief Justice, we object."

Now a Senate roll call was required. From then on throughout the days that Sherman was on the witness stand, almost every question by Stanberry was followed by an objection and a roll call. They were days of haggling, and long arguments on both sides, while a thoroughly disgusted general sat there, unable to testify.

Sherman's testimony, because of Ben Butler's constant objections, was of little importance in the trial record. But his appearance on the witness stand had a definite effect on the Senate, an effect favorable to the defense. About all Sherman was allowed to testify was that Andrew Johnson had asked him to be Secretary of War. But that was enough to make the senators do some hard thinking. Would the House have dared to pass the Tenure Act if the country had known that its passage would keep its hero, Sherman, from heading the War Department? Would the Senate now be trying Andrew Johnson for violating the Tenure Act if Sherman were his Secretary of War?

Ben Butler's longest and loudest objection came when Stanberry asked General Sherman, "After the restoration of Mr. Stanton, upon the vote of the Senate, did you form an opinion as to whether the good of the service required another man in the War Office other than Mr. Stanton."

Butler objected before Sherman could answer, and on the roll call the Senate voted 35-15 not to allow the question. But the question had been asked by Stanberry, and the senators knew full well that Stanberry never would have asked the question if he hadn't been sure that the answer would be "Yes."

Now the Radicals were beginning to worry. Although the defense was being beaten on every roll call, the margin of defeat was becoming narrower. At the beginning of the trial, the vote was four to one against the defense managers. Now the last roll call was little better than two to one for the prosecution. That margin was not enough to convict a President.

On Tuesday morning, April 15, there came the worst blow to the defense thus far in the trial. When the Senate convened that morning, defense manager Evarts rose and announced the illness of Henry Stanberry. Evarts said that Stanberry's physician had ordered him to bed for at least forty-eight hours. Evarts pleaded, "The gentlemen of the

Senate will be so good as to bear in mind that much of the evidence to be produced is within the personal knowledge of Mr. Stanberry, and not within our own."

The Senate adjourned until the next day, but now Stanberry's physician said that he must stay in bed for a week. The defense asked for another delay, but it was refused, and Evarts took over the chairmanship of the Johnson managers.

The situation was now serious for Andrew Johnson. While Ben Butler had shared the burden of prosecution with managers Boutwell and Bingham, Stanberry had carried the ball alone. He had planned the defense strategy. He had interviewed the witnesses for the defense, and only he knew what questions he would ask them. Only he knew what documents the defense would enter as exhibits. He was the only one of the defense managers who had constantly conferred with Andrew Johnson. And now came the final blow. Henry Stanberry had developed pneumonia, and might not live. In any event, he probably could never return to the trial.

Evarts stalled for two days, killing time by introducing as evidence stacks of War Department documents which had little or nothing to do with Andrew Johnson. Then Evarts called his first witness, Walter Cox, a Washington lawyer whom the President had retained to defend General Thomas after Stanton had him hauled before the District of Columbia Municipal Court. Again, Ben Butler poured forth his repeated objections. But now the defense was beginning to win roll calls on the admissibility of evidence.

Cox testified that he had asked the District of Columbia

judge to put General Thomas in a cell, so he could get a write of *habeas corpus*, and prepare for trial. Thomas was put in a cell, but then, Cox said, the judge apparently "got the word" that Thomas was to be released. It was Cox's opinion that Secretary Stanton wanted anything but a trial. Cox's testimony was damaging to the prosecution, and Evarts was rising to the occasion, with none of the timidity he had exhibited when Stanberry was taken ill.

A lawyer named Merrick followed Cox. He also had been engaged by Andrew Johnson to defend Thomas. He confirmed Cox's testimony that Stanton had insisted that Thomas was not to be held in custody. Merrick had said to the judge, "If he is not in custody, he is discharged?" And the judge had replied, "He is discharged."

At this point, Ben Butler lost control of himself. He was beginning to crack emotionally. In objecting to a question by Evarts, he suddenly launched into a lengthy, irrelevant blast against the Johnson administration and its "coddling of the South." He ranted, "While we are waiting for the Attorney General [Stanberry] to get well, numbers of our fellow citizens are being murdered day by day. There is not a man here who does not know that the moment justice is done on this great criminal [Johnson] these murders will cease. Mr. Chief Justice, in Alabama, your register of bankruptcy, appointed by yourself, is today driven from his duties and his home by the Ku Klux Klan, and I have evidence of it lying here on the table. While we are being courteous [to the defense!] the true Union men of the South are being murdered. . . . I say nothing of the threats of assassination against the lives of the great officers of the

Senate, and against the managers. We have not the slightest fear of these cowardly libels on our government, or of these cowardly menaces. All these will go away when this man goes out of the White House."

Ben Butler had gone too far for the senators. The next morning, on a one-sided voice vote, the Senate ruled that Butler's harangue should be stricken from the record of the trial.

That same morning, Evarts drew his ace from the hole when he placed on the witness stand Secretary of the Navy Gideon Welles. The bearded former newspaper editor was the only Cabinet member to testify during the trial. Appointed by Lincoln on the same date as Stanton, Welles had become a world figure through his successful blockade of a coast stretching from Norfolk, Virginia, to the Mexican border. He had created a great navy of steam-powered ironclad ships, where before there had been only a few old wooden sailing ships. The highlight of Welles's testimony was that on the afternoon of last February 21, Andrew Johnson had called a Cabinet meeting. At the close of the meeting, the President announced that he had removed Secretary Stanton and appointed General Thomas to the post. Johnson had described how Thomas had served the removal papers on Stanton, and said that Stanton had agreed to leave the office as soon as he could remove his papers. Welles testified that the Cabinet was in agreement that Stanton must go.

Now Evarts fired his biggest gun. He asked Welles if after Congress had passed the Tenure Act, and the Senate had reinstated Stanton to the War Department, Johnson

had discussed the Act with his Cabinet. "Oh yes," said
Welles, "the President had read it to the Cabinet at the first
meeting after its enactment, and had asked the Cabinet for
advice." Welles said that the Cabinet was in unanimous
agreement that the Act was unconstitutional, and advised
Johnson to veto it. Then Johnson said that, since he was
not a lawyer, he would like help in writing the veto message. Normally such a task would fall on Attorney General
Stanberry, but he was busy with a number of cases before
the Supreme Court. Therefore, the Cabinet chose to help
the President two of its most eminent lawyers, Secretary
of State William Seward, and *Secretary of War Edwin M.
Stanton.*

Now the Radical senators and the prosecution managers
were thoroughly rocked. Was this disloyal, erratic, unpredictable Stanton trying to make them look ridiculous before the nation? So Stanton had helped write the message
which had vetoed the act Congress had passed to keep
Stanton in office! The Radicals were now saying to themselves that the ungrateful Stanton was even worse than
Andrew Johnson made him out to be. But they had spent
over two months of trial in defending Stanton, and they
could not admit that they had been wrong.

Ben Butler spent the rest of the day arguing against admitting Welles's testimony. The next day, April 18, the
Senate voted as usual that Welles's testimony was inad-
missible. Ben Butler had won a tactical victory, but Gideon
Welles had been heard, and he had made the impression
Evarts desired. Welles's testimony might be barred from the
recorded evidence of the trial, but it could not be barred
from the ears of the senators.

With the ten-strike delivered by Secretary Welles, and after entering a bundle of wordy documents as trial exhibits, manager Evarts closed the case for the defense. The Senate adjourned until April 22, when it would hear the final arguments.

✠✠

12 · THE NINTH INNING

That man is a master at punishing himself was ably demonstrated by the United States Senate before its adjournment
to hear the summations of the prosecution and the defense.
Just after manager Evarts closed his case, a resolution was
passed providing that two managers on each side, instead
of the customary one, could be heard in the summations.
Remembering that Ben Butler alone had taken three long
hours to open his prosecution, the senators should have
known what lay ahead.

But the Radicals had a method in their seeming madness.
The oratory was on the side of the prosecution. None of
the defense managers were brilliant speakers, and they
wouldn't have Judge Stanberry to help them. The Radicals
realized that the evidence for the prosecution was weak,

and that little had been actually proved. Thus their only remaining hope was that fire-eating Ben Butler and "Black Jack" Logan might be able to arouse emotions which would bring the conviction of Andrew Johnson.

On the morning of April 22, after Chief Justice Chase had called the Senate to order, "Black Jack" Logan rose to open the summation for the prosecution. "Black Jack," so nicknamed because of his fierce, black mustache, and his mane of raven hair, was the idol of the Grand Army of the Republic which he had founded, the greatest veterans' lobby in American history. He had been a Democratic politician before the War, but now was one of the most vehement Radicals.

As was the custom of the day, Logan opened his speech with calm and extreme modesty. He said, "When one in public life is suddenly called to the discharge of a novel and important public duty, whose consequences will be great, and whose effects will be historical, he must betray an inordinate self-esteem, and an unpardonable lack of modesty, if he did not at the outset acknowledge his diffidence, and solicit forbearance."

But it didn't take "Black Jack" long to get his fires lit. Soon he was saying about Andrew Johnson: "He has betrayed his countrymen, that he might perpetuate his power, and has sacrificed their interests that he might swell his authority . . . And it is not alone that in his public course he has been shameless and guilty, but that his private conduct has been incendiary and malignant. It is not only that he has notoriously broken the law, but that he has criminally scoffed at the framers of the law."

Following this outburst, Logan lulled the Senate to sleep

Impeachment—The Guard before the War Office

by following Butler's example in tracing the history of impeachment trials through all of British and American history. But he awoke the senators when he began pounding away at Johnson's alleged violation of the Tenure of Office Act. Typical of this section of the speech was this: "I will not stop now to speak of the unmanly and disgraceful attempt made by the President and his Cabinet to trick the General-in-Chief [Grant] into a violation of the law, and to force upon Mr. Stanton the alternative of submitting to removal from office, or resorting to legal proceedings which could not possibly have ended during the present administration. The history of all criminals illustrates a constant struggle between crime and cowardice—the desire to commit the crime, and the fear of the consequences that may follow."

Then Logan turned to the case of Colonel Emory: "I have said that this testimony [Emory's] bears proof upon its face as guilt, but we are not permitted to view it from so narrow a standpoint. There is scarcely a scene or act connected with this remarkable drama of Executive usurpation which does not explain this attempt to alienate a gallant officer from his General-in-Chief, and stamp it as scarcely less infamous than the attempt previously made to alienate the General-in-Chief from the whole loyal people of the land. Sirs, there is not in this naked procuration to violate law but a treasonable attempt to poison the mind of a high army officer to sow dissension, insubordination, and treachery in the army."

Finally, after a speech which covered fifty-three printed pages, "Black Jack" Logan, with his arms spread-eagled, and his black mane waving, concluded: "His [Johnson's]

great aim and purpose has been to subvert law, usurp authority, insult and outrage Congress, reconstruct the rebel
states in the interests of treason, insult the memories of our
heroic dead, outrage the feelings of living men who aided
in saving the Union, and deliver all snatched from the
wreck and ruin into the hands of unrepentant, but by him
pardoned, traitors. We are not doubtful of your verdict.
Andrew Johnson has long since been tried by the whole
people and found guilty, and you can but confirm that
judgment already pronounced by the sovereign American
people!"

Now the galleries expected Ben Butler to rise and even
top the performance of "Black Jack." But "Old Cock-eye"
suddenly left the Senate Chamber, and George Boutwell
rose to speak. It was rumored that Butler was completely
exhausted from the weeks of prosecution, and would not
be seen again until the final roll call on conviction.

Representative George S. Boutwell of Massachusetts was
a businessman by training, but his chief interest was education. After being admitted to the bar, he served eleven years
as secretary to the Massachusetts Board of Education, and
ten years as an overseer of Harvard College. In 1863 he was
elected to Congress. During the impeachment trial, he had
ably replaced Butler in leading the prosecution when the
latter was forced to rest.

After Logan's fifty-three-page speech, there was little
left to be said for the prosecution, but that did not deter
manager Boutwell. His speech ran seventy pages. It occupied one afternoon and most of the next day. Extremely
bored, the Senate now voted to increase the length of its
sessions in order to speed the close of the trial.

Now it was time for the defense summation, and the galleries got another surprise. Arising for the defense was manager Thomas A. R. Nelson. He had not been heard throughout the trial, and little was known about him other than that he was a friend of Andrew Johnson, and a Tennessee lawyer. He had not talked long before the Radicals realized that here was a man to be reckoned with, and they were unhappy. Nelson had none of the pomposity and belligerence of Butler. His presentation was not as learned as that of his brother counsel Evarts, but he hit hard, and hit where it hurt.

After reviewing legal precedents, but confining himself to American legal history, he proceeded to Edwin Stanton and the Tenure of Office Act. Here he made a point which both the prosecution and manager Evarts had overlooked, and which changed the whole aspect of the charge that President Johnson had willfully violated the Act. With cunning timing, Nelson suddenly sprung the trap. Edwin M. Stanton had not been *removed*, he had been *suspended*. General Lorenzo Thomas had not been appointed Secretary of War, he had been appointed Secretary *ad interim*. Edwin M. Stanton had never ceased to be Secretary of War; but, since he was suspended, there was need for an *ad interim* substitute.

Nelson proved to be a master of "change of pace." After a long, dry recitation of previous removals and suspensions in the executive branch of the government, from 1789 to 1868, Nelson suddenly switched to humor. Ridicule is a very powerful weapon, and Nelson proved to be an expert in using it.

He took up the charge that Johnson had encouraged

Thomas to take the War Department by force, if Stanton wouldn't get out. In answer to the charge, Nelson painted a picture of the scene between Thomas and Stanton. He began: "There is old General Thomas, a plain, simple-hearted, honest old gentleman who has been forty years in the service of his country. Perhaps his vanity was a little tickled by being appointed Secretary of War.

"He goes to the War Department, and you have that wonderful scene when he attempts to take possession of the office of Secretary of War. This he was going to do by force and violence. Was there ever such an act of force and violence as you had there between Mr. Thomas and Mr. Stanton? [laughter] They met like twin brothers. I believe Mr. Thomas said Mr. Stanton did hug him. In the fullness of his heart, Mr. Stanton became extremely kind, and he called for liquor. It was equally divided between the two Secretaries of War, and done in a spirit of fraternity and love such as I suppose was never witnessed in a forcible contest on the face of the earth before [more laughter].

"And they tell you that this was force! Oh yes, force—attempting to forcibly eject Mr. Stanton from the office of Secretary of War by drinking a bottle of liquor with him. Was there ever such an idea of force before? This is the lame and impotent conclusion of the proceedings which we have on the other side."

Then Nelson proceeded to the matter of Colonel Emory. In discussing Andrew Johnson's concern about the number of troops stationed in the nation's capital, Nelson proved that he not only had a sense of humor, but also colossal nerve. In 1868, a speaker casting aspersions on the Grand Army of the Republic would make as many friends as a

Cartoon—*King Andy I*

speaker in 1964 suggesting that the American Legion is a communist-front organization. But Nelson took the bit in his teeth: "The G.A.R. seemed to be figuring upon a large-scale operation, and if there had not been great prudence on the part of Congress, and very great prudence on the part of the President, we should have had this country again enveloped in civil war. . . . In this state of things, when the whole country was agitated . . . when men's minds were aroused everywhere in the unfortunate division of parties in the United States to such an extent that they were offering troops on one hand to sustain the Congress, and troops on the other hand to maintain the President, and when the General of the Armies and the President differed in their opinions, I maintain that the very fact that the President has done nothing of a military character shows that he had no intentions to do the acts which are imputed to him. . . . How did he know that General Grant might not be endeavoring to envelop, to surround him by troops, and have him arrested? Had he not a right to inquire into the introduction of these military forces here?"

Next Nelson turned to Johnson's speeches in Cleveland and St. Louis. These he disposed of by maintaining that the President had the same right as any private citizen to express his views. He said in part, "I say that these speeches were not official, like his messages to Congress, but were private and personal, and in answer to the call of his fellow citizens. . . . Members of Congress have the right to speak with perfect freedom of the conduct of the President, and the President in turn has the right to 'carry the war to Africa,' and speak about Congress whenever he is assailed. . . . I maintain that when Andrew Johnson makes a tour from Washington to Chicago, Cleveland, and St. Louis, and returns to this city, he is nothing but a private citizen."

In closing, Nelson made a sentimental appeal to the conscience of the Senate: "And when the day shall come—and may it be far distant—when each of you shall 'shuffle off this mortal coil,' may no thorn be planted in the pillow of death to embitter your recollection of the scene that is being enacted now; and when the time shall come, as it may in some future age, when your own spirits shall flit among the hoary columns and chambers of this edifice, may each of you then be enabled to exclaim *'Here I faithfully discharged the highest duty of earth; here I nobly discarded all passion, prejudice, and feeling; here I did my whole duty, regardless of consequences; and here I find my own name inscribed in letters of gold, flashing and shining, upon the immortal rolls where the names of all just men and true patriots are recorded.'"*

Defense manager Nelson sat down. The fate of President Andrew Johnson now rested in the hands of fifty-four United States Senators.

13 · THE FINAL ROLL CALL

If the pall of impeachment which hung over Andrew Johnson made any impression on him, it was not evident that April of 1868. The social life at the White House was gayer than ever. Mrs. Johnson was now an invalid, and never appeared in public, but the President's two charming daughters served as hostesses. The President frequently attended parties in private homes, and often took carriage rides in Rock Creek Park.

But at the other end of Pennsylvania Avenue confusion reigned, nerves frayed, and tempers grew short. The Radicals were now determined to delay the final count on conviction as long as possible. Their nose counts after the last Senate roll calls had not been encouraging. Now they needed time to reorganize their ranks and plan new strategy.

They had to get "the folks back home" to pressure their senators. Support from state governors and political bosses had to be enlisted. The wayward senators had to be impressed with the idea that it would be political suicide to vote against the conviction of the President. The G.A.R. had to be alerted.

Now, to kill time, all of the managers were permitted to make summations. Their speeches were endless repetitions of everything that had been said by Logan and Nelson. Judge Stanberry had recovered from his illness, and was allowed to speak. The speeches lasted from April 25 through May 7. Because the senators were bored and exhausted, Chief Justice Chase had difficulty in maintaining a quorum. Nerves began to crack. At one point, defense manager Nelson, infuriated by Ben Butler's badgering, exploded, and earned a vote of censure for "using language offensive to the United States Senate." At the conclusion of prosecution manager Bingham's speech, a crowd of Radical supporters cheered so loudly that Chief Justice Chase was forced to order the Sergeant-at-arms and his aides to clear the galleries. This nearly created an incident, since the Sergeant-at-arms, taking the Chief Justice literally, also cleared the diplomatic and press galleries.

There came another long delay caused by disagreement over how and when the final vote should be held. The Democrats wanted to ballot immediately, but the Radicals staved them off. There was debate as to whether the House should be invited to witness the final roll calls. It was voted that they should. A motion was made that the final vote be taken on Monday, May 11, but it was defeated 37-13.

On Monday the Senate voted to hold the final roll call on Wednesday. Then on Tuesday, Senator "Zack" Chandler of Michigan announced that his colleague, Senator Howard, was very ill, and that attending a roll call might imperil his life. Chandler moved postponement of the roll call to Saturday, May 16, and his motion was carried.

Now it was Saturday. Was this to be the fateful day? It appeared that it was, as Chief Justice Chase instructed the Clerk of the Senate, and the Sergeant-at-arms to proceed, and escort the members of the House to the Senate Chamber. The galleries were packed, and they were policed against any possible demonstration.

The members of the House expectantly entered the Senate Chamber. Thad Stevens, now near death, was carried to his seat at the prosecution managers' table. Then there was a hush as Senator Howard of Michigan was brought in on a stretcher. A test roll call was taken to see that all senators were present, and it was found that Senator Grimes of Iowa was absent. The Radicals moved for adjournment, but just then Grimes entered and took his seat. They started with the passage of a resolution which provided for each article of impeachment to be voted on separately, beginning with Article XI, the "Stanton Article."

Now the moment had surely come. Chief Justice Chase, looking more awesome than ever, rapped with his gavel and announced, "By direction of the Senate the Chief Justice admonishes the citizens and strangers in the galleries that absolute silence and perfect order are required. It will be a matter of unfeigned regret if any violation of the order of the Senate should necessitate the execution of its further order, that the persons guilty of disturbance be immediately arrested.

"Senators, in conformity with the order of the Senate, the Chair will now proceed to take the vote on the eleventh article. The Clerk will first read the eleventh article."

Now the air in the Senate Chamber fairly crackled with tension as the Senate clerk read, laid down the eleventh article, and called, "Mr. Anthony."

The Rhode Island senator rose, and Chief Justice Chase asked, "How say you, Mr. Senator Anthony? Is the respondent, Andrew Johnson, President of the United States, guilty or not guilty of a high misdemeanor, as charged in this article?"

Senator Anthony: "Guilty."

Senator Bayard was next with "Not guilty," and so it went through the alphabet, and a scowl was on the face of every Radical in the Senate, and in the visiting House. Each member had been keeping his own tally on a pad of paper. Thirty-six votes, two-thirds of the Senate, were necessary to convict, and the Radicals weren't getting that kind of margin.

After Senator Yates of Illinois had completed the alphabet by voting "Guilty," the Clerk tallied his figures, and the count stood: Guilty, 35; Not Guilty, 19—*one vote short of conviction!*

Now Chief Justice Chase instructed the Clerk to read Article I, and proceed with another roll call. But the Radicals demanded that the vote on the first roll call be read. With a margin of one vote, there could have been a mistake, they said. Then a Radical senator moved for a fifteen-

minute recess, thinking that it might provide enough time
to threaten or cajole one senator into changing his vote.
The motion to recess was voted down, and Chief Justice
Chase announced that he would read the results of no roll
calls until all of the articles had been voted on, unless a
motion of the Senate so instructed him. The motion was
passed, and the Chief Justice announced, "Upon this article,
thirty-five senators vote 'Guilty,' and nineteen senators
vote 'Not guilty.' Two-thirds of the senators not having
pronounced 'Guilty,' the President is therefore acquitted
upon this article."

The Radicals had lost round one, but there were ten articles to go, and all they needed, they thought, was *time* to
change one vote. After a hurried conference with his col-
leagues, Senator Williams of Oregon moved that the Senate
adjourn until Tuesday, the twenty-sixth (it was now Saturday). Minority Leader Hendricks of Indiana entered a
strong protest. When in a court of law, he asked, would a
jury, trying the most important case in American history,
be allowed to run loose all over Washington, in bars, hotel
lobbies, and boarding-houses, before reaching a verdict?
But although the Radicals had failed to produce the necessary thirty-six votes to convict the President, they still had
a majority, and the Senate adjourned until Tuesday.

Never was there a weekend of more furious politicking
in Washington. Thirty-five senators and three-quarters of
the House were working to change at least one vote. Ben
Butler said of a senator under pressure, "Tell the damn
scoundrel that if he wants money, there is a bushel of it
to be had."

In the lobby of the Willard Hotel, a man was waving

Impeachment of the President

The rift between President Johnson and the Radical Republican Congress had been steadily widening. In 1867 the Tenure-of-Office Act, designed to keep Secretary of War Stanton in office, had been passed over the President's veto.

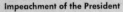

U. S. SENATE

№.

To be taken up at MAIN ENTRANCE

U. S. SENATE

U.S.SENATE

Impeachment President

ADMIT THE BEARER

MARCH 13. 1868

Geo. T. Brown
Sergeant-at-Arms.

Johnson removed Stanton, and the House of Representatives, dominated by the Radicals, voted for impeachment. The trial opened on Mar. 13, 1868.

Harper's Weekly, Apr. 4, 1868

In accordance with the Constitution the Senate sat as a court and was presided over by the Chief Justice of the Supreme Court. *Opposite* is a view of the opening of the trial.

Frank Leslie's Illustrated Newspaper, Mar. 28, 1868

Frank Leslie's Illustrated Newspaper, Jun. 6, 1868
Taking the Vote, May 16, 1868

On May 16 the first vote was taken. Thirty-five Senators voted for conviction; nineteen for acquittal. Two-thirds were required for conviction. By one vote the President was saved from impeachment. Subsequent votes gave the same numbers for and against. The court adjourned and did not again convene. Thus failed the first attempt to impeach a President of the United States.

6525 v 5

Scenes from the Impeachment Hearings

five hundred dollars in bills, offering to bet that Johnson would be convicted. General Grant had been given a list of senators to call on, most of them former army men. As the weekend progressed, the fears of the Radicals increased. There was a rumor that Senator Frelinghuysen of New Jersey was switching to "Not guilty." But there was a ray of hope. Senator Grimes, who had voted for acquittal, had been taken ill.

Now the Radicals' pressure concentrated on Ross of Kansas who had voted "Not guilty." Private detectives followed him day and night. His Kansas colleague, Senator Pomeroy, showed Ross a telegram from a constituent, calling him a skunk. Ross could never hold a public office again in Kansas should he vote for acquittal, Pomeroy told him.

Tuesday noon came, and the outlook was still dark for the Radicals. As soon as the House had solemnly moved into the Senate Chamber, Senator Morrill of Maine moved that the Senate adjourn until June 23, a period of nearly a month. The vote was a tie, 27-27, the largest vote against the Radicals thus far. The Chief Justice, not being President of the Senate, could not vote to break the tie, but he ruled that the motion had not carried.

For some strategic reason not apparent in the records, the Senate voted to proceed with the second article of impeachment. This article accused Johnson of violating the Tenure Act by appointing Lorenzo Thomas Secretary of War. The result of the roll call was the same as Saturday's, 35-19. The Radical ranks had held as a result of the weekend efforts, but the one precious vote hadn't been gained, and Ross of Kansas had remained firm.

The Radicals had two strikes on them. Would there be a third? Delays having proved futile, the Radicals allowed the Senate to proceed with the third article. This article was a minor repetition of the second, emphasizing that Andrew Johnson had appointed Thomas *while the Senate was in session*.

For the third time, the Clerk of the Senate called, "Senator Anthony." Then the Clerk proceeded through the senatorial alphabet, and not a vote was changed. He called, "Senator Ramsey," and, as before, the answer was "Guilty." Now every eye was trained on Edmund G. Ross of Kansas, that is, every eye except one of Ben Butler's. Senator Pomeroy was glaring at Ross and waving in his direction the "skunk telegram" from home. Would Ross dare flout the overwhelming Radical sentiment in his home state? Would he throw away a brilliant political career by uttering two words, instead of enhancing it with one?

The Clerk of the Senate called, "Senator Ross." Ross rose, pressing his lips together. Chief Justice Chase leaned forward and asked slowly, "Mr. Senator Ross, how say you, is the respondent, Andrew Johnson, President of the United States, guilty or not guilty of a high misdemeanor, as charged in this article?"

If anyone had taken a deep breath, it could have been heard from the front row of the Senate to the press gallery. Thad Stevens, who had been barely conscious for the last two days, and who along with Senator Grimes had been carried into the Senate Chamber that day, cupped his hands over both ears.

Edmund Ross was slow to answer, but he lifted his

Thaddeus Stevens being conveyed to the House of Representatives to preside over Johnson's impeachment proceedings

shoulders high, braced himself, took a deep breath, and then replied in a loud, clear voice, "Not guilty."

The Radicals knew then what to expect, and they got it, the same 35-19 vote. They were whipped. There was no point in voting on the other articles. Andrew Johnson had been acquitted of the three strongest charges. The rest might be beaten even worse. After a trial lasting three months, the testimony and exhibits of which would fill three fat volumes when printed, and after wearing out twelve of the nation's best lawyers, the United States Senate had refused to admit before the world that in our American democracy, the people cannot be trusted to elect a man to the Vice Presidency who is fit to be President.

In response to several nodding Radical heads, Senator Williams of Oregon rose and moved that the Senate adjourn *sine die* (literally "without day," or until the opening of the Fortieth Congress). The vote was 34-16, and the trial of Andrew Johnson, our only President to be impeached, was over.

That afternoon, Andrew Johnson went for his customary ride in Rock Creek Park. There, he stopped beside the Creek and reminisced about that afternoon in April, 1865, when he had just left the funeral train of Abraham Lincoln. History cannot record people's thoughts, or what they say to themselves. But at that moment it is almost certain that Andrew Johnson said, "Yes, Mr. President, I *tried* to carry it out—to the letter."

That night there was a party at the White House. Among the guests were "the gallant nineteen" who had stood by Andrew Johnson through the three fateful roll calls. The Marine Band was there to play for dancing. It had played two quadrilles when the chief usher announced, "Ladies and Gentlemen—the President of the United States." The Marine Band struck up *Hail to the Chief*. Then entered a very happy, smiling, ex-tailor from Greenville, Tennessee, with a beautiful daughter on each arm.

∞∞∞

POSTLUDE

During the 1960 Presidential campaign, several newspaper columnists and television commentators discussed the idea that should either John F. Kennedy or Richard M. Nixon be elected and serve two terms, they would still be too young to retire from important government service. Unlike Truman and Eisenhower, they just could not retire and play the roles of elder statesmen. But with the Presidency behind them, what could they do? These political analysts pointed to John Quincy Adams as the only former President who returned to Congress after leaving the White House. In this they were in error.

After serving the unexpired term of Abraham Lincoln, Andrew Johnson vacated the White House for Ulysses S. Grant, and returned to Tennessee. There he was no longer the renegade Southern Democrat. He was now a hero who had done his best to carry out the humane, reasonable Reconstruction of Abraham Lincoln. Soon Johnson received a call from the Democratic State Committee. Their spokesman hesitantly asked, "Mr. Johnson, we know it would be a come-down after being President, but Tennessee needs you, the South needs you, and the Democratic Party needs you. Won't you run for the Senate?" To such an appeal, Andrew Johnson could have only one answer.

Back at his old desk in the United States Senate, Andrew Johnson served with dignity, humility, and humanity. And he never forgot his pledge to Abraham Lincoln: "Yes, Mr. President, I swear before God that I will carry it out—to the letter."

BIBLIOGRAPHY

Barnes, W. H., *History of the Thirty-ninth Congress.*
New York: Harper & Brothers, 1868
Bowers, Claude G., *The Tragic Era.* Boston: Houghton
Mifflin, 1929
Buckmaster, Henrietta, *Let My People Go.* New York:
Harper & Brothers, 1941
Butler, Benjamin F., *Butler's Book.* Boston: A. M. Thayer,
1892
Carter, Hodding, *The Angry Scar.* New York: Doubleday
& Co., Inc., 1959
Chaplin, Jeremiah and J. D., *Life of Charles Sumner.* Bos-
ton: D. Lothrop Co., 1874
Davis, Varina Howell, *Jefferson Davis, Ex-President of the
Confederate States* (2 vol.). New York: Bedford Co.,
1890

Grant, Ulysses S., *Personal Memoirs of U.S. Grant* (2 vol.). Montreal: Dawson Brothers, 1886

Leech, Margaret, *Reveille in Washington.* New York: Harper & Brothers, 1941

Logan, John A., *The Great Conspiracy.* New York: A. R. Hart & Co., 1886

Moore, Ben: Perley, *Perley's Reminiscences of Sixty Years in the National Metropolis* (2 vol.). Philadelphia: Hubbard Brothers, 1886

Schucker, J. W., *The Life of Salmon P. Chase.* New York: D. Appleton & Co., 1874

Stephens, Alexander H., *A Constitutional View on the War Between the States* (2 vol.). National Publishing Co., 1868

Thomas, Maj. Gen. George H., *Memoir of Maj. Gen. George H. Thomas.* Philadelphia: J. B. Lippincott & Co., 1881

U.S. Government Printing Office, *Trial of Andrew Johnson, Published by Order of the Senate* (3 vol.). Washington, D.C.: 1868

West, Richard S., Jr., *Gideon Welles, Lincoln's Navy Department.* New York: Bobbs-Merrill Co., 1943

INDEX

DATE DUE

30 505 JOSTEN'S